PROFIT SEASONS

HARVESTING DOLLARS WITH OPTIONS ON SEASONAL AGRICULTURAL COMMODITIES

C.D. KING

Contents

This book is dedicated to my wonderful, kind and brilliant husband, Herbert King, the city farmer who always has a good idea, and to my kind and loving parents, Garland and Margaret Wiley, two of the finest people that I have ever known.

Introduction

In today's world of stocks, NFTs, cryptocurrency and an unstable real estate market, it is becoming harder and harder to know what to invest in and what to forgo. Let's be honest, we all want to invest! We all want to make returns on our investments and see our portfolio grow (whether as a side income or a full time income). But, with so much information and advice out there, from so many different voices, it can be difficult to know where to even begin.

As a beginner, the investment market can appear deliberately complicated to keep those who are not in the know out. Numbers, figures, percentages and extremely technical language can all seem headache-inducing, putting off even the most dedicated of economic-enthusiasts. Moreover, for many beginners, you may not even be aware of the investment options available to you. Unfortunately, financial literacy is not taught in schools, leaving most economic-enthusiasts in the dark about *how* to invest.

There is good news, nevertheless! For those traders just starting out in commodity trading, this book has been written to bring some light to formerly obfuscated trading knowledge. If you are a trader who would like to have a basic understanding of the factors which influence the profit of seasonal crops, then this book has been written just for you! If you would like to have a basic understanding of how commodity options function and if you would like to gain a greater understanding of the factors which influence the profit of seasonal crops, then this book has been written specifically for you. It covers the who, what, when, where and how of the basics of options commodity trading with seasonals.

As a beginner to the world of agricultural commodities*, you may be wondering where to begin? You may have heard specific industry jargon that left you feeling confused and even more in the dark about agricultural commodities. What do "futures" mean? What are commodities? What are the practical steps you need to take to trade them? How do you make profit from trading them? You naturally have a lot of questions about the industry that need answers. At the same time, you understand that there is profit to be made if you play your cards right. So, you naturally want to learn everything that a beginner needs to know, in a simple, concise and easy-to-understand language.

In this book, you will learn the fundamentals of agricultural commodities trading, including:

- The economic history of futures and options.
- How option contracts and future contracts work.
- The differences between futures and options and which better suit your financial and investment needs.
- The differences between commodity options and stock options.
- Good options strategies to make financially savvy decisions.
- How to make options trading profitable.
- How to get started trading options.
- How to find a reputable commodity broker.

*In this book, agricultural commodities refer to agricultural products that can be bought and sold. These include things like cotton, dry beans, oats, rye, tobacco, peanuts, wheat, sugar beets, flax, barley, rice, raisins, organes, dry peas, canning and freezing peas, potatoes, grain sorghum, tomatoes, soybeans, nursery crops, apples, forests and timer, grapes, tame hay, nuts, hemp and native grass. Agricultural commodities also include aquacultural species, such as aquatic invertebrates (eg. mollusk, finfish and crustaceans), reptiles, amphibians and aquatic plants, such as kelp.

How To Use This Book

1. As a beginner, you may be unfamiliar with some of the financial jargon used in this book. As a result, I have created a useful, alphabetical index at the end of this book to guide you through the many financial terms that you may not understand. These terms have been marked with asterisks in the text, so that you can easily spot them.

2. Using futures and options contracts, whether separately or in combination, can offer you numerous trading opportunities. However, the strategies in this guide are not intended to be used as a complete and foolproof guide to every possible trading strategy. Rather, they are a starting point, helping you take the first steps into the world of futures trading . Whether the contents will prove to be the best strategies and steps for you depends on other factors not controlled for by the information in this book, such as your knowledge of the market, how much risk your commodities/assets carry and your commodity trading objectives.

3. I encourage you to highlight important parts of this book so that you can go back in case you need to revisit advice specific to your investments and financial decisions.

So if you're ready to harvest dollars with options on seasonal agricultural commodities, then settle in with this book and get ready to open the world to bigger financial options and greater financial independence.

Chapter 1

Introduction To Futures

Despite being much more volatile and unpredictable, agricultural commodities are a hot asset in today's financial market. In fact, the market is ever-growing today as an investment option for anyone brave enough to open their economic opportunities. Since futures contracts are not as popular as the traditional stock market, it has traditionally put people off from trading on the market. However, for those who trade in futures, being able to predict the economic future is another added advantage. For example, the price of a barrel* of crude oil on your futures contract is a great predictor of the stock market in the future, since higher gas prices on the futures contracts equals higher cost of food, manufacturing and so on. This chapter will discuss the pros and cons of futures trading in greater detail later.

In the words of Adam Hickerson, Manager, Futures and Forex, TD Ameritrade: "Futures have such a robust market. There are so many different parties and individuals trading futures, who combined provide access to deep liquidity*, making it easier for all participants to conduct business and trade." (**Source**) So what exactly are futures contracts?

What Are Futures Contracts?

A futures contract is what it says on the tin. It is a contract that allows you to legally buy and sell agricultural assets in the future. These prices of these assets are set before the date of purchase or of sale and a specific time is set where you can then buy or sell these agricultural commodities. A futures contract has a few similarities to stock trading. For instance, like stocks, you will need to purchase your futures contracts on an exchange group. Just as you can purchase stock on the New York Stock Exchange, you can purchase future contracts electronically on futures exchange groups, for example the CME Group (Chicago Mercantile Exchange Group)

Futures contracts are very detailed and standardized to ensure that everything is as fair as possible. When you purchase a contract, it will include very specific information. This includes:

- The unit pricing of your asset. If you want to buy soybean futures for example, then your contract may state that you are purchasing 5,000 bushels* (or 136 metric tons) of soybeans.
- The minimum price difference between the price agreed on at the time of the bid and the price of the asset (set by the futures exchange group) at any particular day or time. This is the minimum price fluctuation you can expect on your asset value, known as the tick size.
- The quantity of the assets you want to purchase.
- The quality of the assets you want to purchase.
- The date and location of your delivery - although most agricultural commodities are not often delivered physically, because the contracts are often liquidated (meaning that cash is transferred) rather than delivered.
- Details of non-physical delivery*.

To truly understand how futures contracts work, it is best to go back to the beginning, i.e. its history. In essence, to understand how they work, we must first understand how the industry began.

How Futures Began

One of the earliest records of the futures market is found in Japan in the early 1700s, when people traded rice as contracts for profit. In fact, Japan's Osaka Dojima Commodity Exchange, which began in 1730, is set to see its last trade in June 2022 (Reuters, 2021). The Osaka Dojima Commodity Exchange began after samurais "petitioned the Tokugawa shogunate to authorize trade in rice futures at the Dojima Exchange" as a way to protect their wealth, which was tied into rice (Reuters, 2021). The dojima Exchange would greatly influence trade rules and practices that are used in commodity, equities and financial futures exchanges (Reuters, 2021).

More than a century after the Osaka Dojima Commodity Exchange began, The Chicago Board of Trade (CBOT) was established in 1848 by grain merchants. The CBOT was the first grain futures exchange in the United States and would later become one of the world's largest futures markets (Encyclopaedia Britannica, 2022). In 2007, the CBOT merged with Chicago Mercantile Exchange Holdings Inc which trades futures exchange and options (Encyclopaedia Britannica, 2022). This merger would become CME Group Inc. Later, in 2015, CME Group Inc. would swap out in-person trade of futures contracts (in the trading pit) with online trading (Encyclopaedia Britannica, 2022).

Writing on the history of the CBOT, Marketswiki, a derivatives market database, writes: "Farmers raised livestock and grew crops and other agricultural commodities and brought them to market to sell to commercial entities. Substantial risk existed on both sides of that process. Buyers were vulnerable to the delivery of substandard products, or no products at all if the growing season had failed to produce enough of the commodity. [Buyers] needed

3

a way to ensure that the quantity and quality of commodity they needed would be available when they needed it. Farmers needed a way to know that a glut of available crops would not put them out of business" (Blythe, 2018). Hence, to mitigate these risks on both sides of the process, contracts are very detailed, including information on quantity, quality, delivery date and so on.

How Futures Contracts Work

Futures contracts are <u>derivatives</u>*. A futures contract obligates one party to transact a particular asset (or assets) at a predetermined date and time and for a predetermined price. The price of an asset in a futures contract is determined not by the price of the asset at the expiration date, but at the time the contract is signed. This is why a futures contract includes the <u>tick size</u>* of the asset(s).

The volatility of a futures contract comes from the set price which cannot be changed once the contract expires (and the transaction has to be fulfilled). This means that, if I purchase 500 bushels of oats and the price rises by 20% at the expiration date, I will not be paying for the 20% increase, thereby making a profit. On the other hand, it also means that if the prices of oats decrease by 40% at the expiration date, I will be making a significant loss. If I am the farmer/trader selling my oats, a futures contract guarantees that I "lock in" the price of my commodity or asset. In essence, I can sell my commodity even before it is ready, giving me financial peace of mind. On the other hand, I take a big risk because the price of oats may rise significantly after I sign the futures contract. Of course, if the price decreases significantly, then I enjoy the rewards of taking a big risk that has worked out in my favor.

Futures contracts, also known as futures, do not have to be agricultural commodities alone. There are a few other types of futures contracts. They are:

- Commodity futures. These include products that come from the earth, usually in unrefined or partially-refined states. Examples are agricultural commodities, like oats and soybeans, and other commodities, such as crude oil and natural gas.
- Precious and industrial metal futures. These include all metals which fall under these two categories, such as gold, silver and copper, found in mining deposits. Precious and industrial metal futures allow you to invest in the metal industry.
- Stock index futures. These are traded in national and international stock markets all over the world, for example the FTSE 100 Index, the Hang Seng Index or the Swiss Market Index. Stock index futures allow you to purchase shares in a business or company. This way, you gain a profit when the business gains a profit, but lose on your investment when the business makes a loss.
- Currency futures. Currency futures determine the price in which currencies all over the world are bought and sold at a fixed exchange rate, for a specific date in the future (the expiration date).
- U.S. treasury futures. These are standardized features contracts, where you can buy or sell U.S. government notes or bonds.

When you purchase a futures contract, the underlying asset* you acquired becomes your possession once the contract expires. This is known as the expiration date. Alternatively, you can choose to take the cash equivalent rather than the asset. You can, however, choose to sell your position in the contract before the expiration date. This is similar to American-style options contracts, where you can buy and sell your asset even before the expiration date of the contract. European-style options contracts only allow for you to buy and sell after the expiration date (**see Chapter Two**).

How Margin is Used in Futures Exchanges

As with any other type of trading, the trading of futures is done through financial exchange. Although futures exchanges are now done electronically, it was originally carried out on the trading floor of the Chicago Board of Trade (CBOT), as well as other exchanges in what was known as outcry trading. Before we explain how margins are used in futures exchanges, it is important to understand one of the critical functions of exchanges: to secure a futures contract for both parties, ensuring that all contracts are guaranteed. This means that neither buyer nor seller can back out once the contract has been agreed upon. Futures exchanges eliminate risk for both parties, guaranteeing that the futures market remains trustworthy and well-respected among investors.

So how is margin used in futures exchanges? When making general stock investments, you buy on margin by borrowing money from your broker. This is essentially a loan from your brokerage firm that gives you more buying power to purchase more stock. As a result, you are able to make a bigger investment than you would have been able to afford. The general idea is to make the purchase of stocks more effective for investors. In futures exchanges, you can purchase on margin by putting down a "good faith" deposit. This good faith deposit is the initial margin requirement. Also known as a performance bond, the margin is a guarantee from both the seller and buyer that they will legally fulfil the contract and all its obligations.

As an investor who wants to trade in futures contracts, you will need to open an account with a futures commission merchant (FCM) and then post the initial margin requirement for the contract. You will be able to find the initial margin requirement of the futures contract you want to enter into at the exchange's clearing house*. In fact, the exchange sets margin requirements for each futures product. Each futures commodity has its own set of risk dynamics, so the initial margin requirement is decided based on the commodity you want to purchase, market volatility* and the brokerage firm's terms and conditions. It is also typically just a small percentage of the contract's notional value*.

If the price of the commodity rises during the time, the broker will produce a margin call. A margin call will require that you add more funds to your trader account. You will have a specific time period to add funds to your trader's account. If you miss this deadline then your investment will be liquidated. Nonetheless, despite this one disadvantage, margins make futures a very capital-efficient way to expand the types of markets in which you can invest, opening you up to other types of assets, such as commodities, currencies, equity indices and interest rates.

How Do You Use Futures?

You will have to learn how to use futures if you want to make a profit. After all, it is imperative that you know how a market works before investing in it. So how do you use futures?

Typically, futures contracts are bought using leverage*. With leverage, you do not need to pay for 100% of the underlying asset's value. The broker* and the seller will ask for an initial margin amount* that is a fraction of the asset's value. Think of it as putting a downpayment for a home or a car. Just like any down payment, the amount you put down is based on a few conditions, such as the full value of the assets, your credit history and even the seller's and broker's own terms and conditions. The broker can hold up to a certain amount in a margin account. This amount is dependent on how creditworthy you are, how much the broker themselves want to take and the size of the contract.

All futures contracts can either be physically delivered or cash-settled. For those who invest in agricultural commodities, you may decide you want the 400 bushels of oats delivered to you. A company that makes breakfast bars will want their oats delivered to them once the expiration date is reached. Usually, when a buyer wants to ensure their asset will be delivered, they hedge* the price

7

of the commodity they need, ensuring they don't have to pay more later on. Conversely, if you are a private trader, speculating* on the trade market, then you will net the difference between your original trade price and the closing trade price. This net difference is then returned to you as a cash settlement. In this case, your commodity futures contract works similarly to a stock index futures contract.

When speculating on your futures contract, you can offset or unwound your purchase (the long position*) by selling for the same amount at the current price. This will then close your long position and the difference between the prices of both contracts becomes cash-settled in the investor's brokerage account. In this case, there is no need for physical products to change hands. Speculating on your future's contract is risky because you could end up making a loss if your commodity's price was lower than the purchase price in your original futures contract. If it is higher, however, you stand to make a lot of profit.

Holding a Futures Contract Until Expiration

If you hold a futures contract until expiration, your position is settled on cash, meaning that you receive a cash settlement for your underlying asset. This cash settlement is dependent on whether or not your underlying asset saw a decrease or increase in value during the period when you were holding it (as discussed in the **contract example** given below). If you held your contract until expiration and you chose to have it delivered, you suddenly become the owner of the commodity. That means that you are now responsible for said commodities, including handling and storage, as well as insurance.

Stakeholders In A Futures Contract

Although this chapter has mostly focused on the buyer and seller of a futures contract (and futures assets), there are other stakeholders in a futures contract that allow money to move and investments to be a success. Stakeholders have different reasons for buying and selling futures contracts or for working in the industry. The broker/brokerage firm is the most obvious stakeholder as they are the most immediate intermediary between the buyer and the seller. Other stakeholders include the government (who regulates the industry) and farmers, who often sell their commodities to companies looking to speculate and purchase commodities at a cheaper price than is sold on the regular market. There are also retail traders, individuals who trade on the market for a living and institutional investors, looking to either speculate or hedge their risk. Lastly, there are also corporations who act as both seller and buyer in the futures market. Other stakeholders include individuals speculating on market fluctuations to make a profit by buying low and selling high, hedge funds and big banks.

Who Trades What?

Futures contracts were originally created for institutional buyers who wanted the commodity delivered so that they could resell the stock to other stakeholders for profit. For example, a dealer would buy 1,000 bushels of wheat on leverage, then resell it to a cereal manufacturer, making a profit based on the increased price of wheat at the time of resale. They were a safer investment bet for buyers because the price of sale/purchase was always determined in advance, reducing the risk of price swings.

Since futures contracts can now be exchanged for a cash settlement, retail buyers often buy/sell futures contracts to make a profit on the commodity's increasing upon expiration, without needing to take possession of said commodity.

Regular trading hours for futures contracts are between 8:30 am and 3:00pm. You can also trade overnight electronically on marketplaces that offer futures and options products. Additionally, you are able to trade some futures products 24/7.

Who Regulates Futures?

Futures markets (in the United States) are regulated by the CFTC (Commodity Futures Trading Commission), a federal agency. Set up in 1974 by Congress, the CFTC regulates market pricing as well as brokerage firms. It ensures that futures buyers and sellers do not participate in abusing the market for their own unethical or illegal gain. This includes fraud and insider trading.

Pros and Cons of Futures

As you would imagine, there are a few pros and cons to futures contracts. They are:

Pros

- You can use your futures contract to speculate on the direction of an underlying asset and, hopefully, make a profit.
- In many instances, futures contracts require just a fraction of the contract amount with the broker.
- Sellers can go into a futures contract to hedge the price of their commodity assets. That way, they mitigate the risk of adverse price increases.

Cons

- Since futures contracts use leverage, you may end up making a loss from your initial margin amount. Although margins have the capacity to bring you profit, when they bring loss, the loss is always significant.
- If you tie your asset to one (or more contracts) through hedging, you may lose on profitable price movements.

- The market is traded online, giving you round-the-clock access to trading, investing and making profits.

Contract Example

Below is a contract example to give you an idea of how a futures contract would work in real life from the time of purchase to the expiration.

You purchase 600 bushels of soybeans, hoping to hedge the price months before harvest, speculating on making a profit once the contract expires after harvest, once soybeans once more become scarce. You purchase the soybeans at $63, its trading price for the month your contract is expected to expire. Rather than pay its full notional value, $37,000, you pay just a small portion (its initial margin).

For the next few months, you watch the price of soybeans fluctuate, directly affecting the price of your futures contract. The price swings are stable, but suddenly become volatile during harvest. You are asked by your broker to provide a maintenance margin to be deposited into your margin account.

At the expiration of your contract, a few months later, soybeans are priced at $87 per bushel. You exit your position* by selling your original contract and cash-settling. You make $14,400 in net profit (minus all commissions and fees). If your speculation ends in loss, however, with the price of soybeans falling to $60 per bushel, you lose $1,800.

Chapter Summary

- Agricultural commodities are a hot asset in today's financial market, albeit a volatile and unpredictable one.
- A futures contract allows you to legally buy and sell agricultural assets in the future.

- To mitigate risks on both sides of the process, futures contracts are very detailed, including information on quantity, quality, delivery date and so on.
- The price of an asset in a futures contract is determined not by the price of the asset at the expiration date, but at the time the contract is signed.
- When you purchase a futures contract, the underlying asset you acquired becomes your possession after the expiration date. If so, your agricultural commodity will be delivered to you. You can also choose to take the cash equivalent rather than the asset.
- When making general stock investments, you buy on margin by borrowing money from your broker.
- To trade in futures contracts, you will need to open an account with a futures commission merchant (FCM) and then post the initial margin requirement for the contract.
- The initial margin requirement is decided based on the commodity you want to purchase, market volatility and the brokerage firm's terms and conditions.
- If the price of the commodity rises before the expiration of your position (your contract), the broker will produce a margin call.
- Futures contracts are bought using leverage.
- Speculating on your future's contract is risky because you could end up making a loss if your commodity's price was lower than the purchase price in your original futures contract. If it is higher, however, you stand to make a lot of profit.
- Futures markets (in the United States) are regulated by the CFTC (Commodity Futures Trading Commission). It ensures that futures buyers and sellers do not participate in abusing the market for their own unethical or illegal gain.

You can see now that a futures contract is a great way to invest with minimal risk, without much capital and with a good probability of making a profit. With the ability to invest online at any time of the day, harvesting dollars with futures is only at the touch of your fingertips. You are now armed with information on how to use futures for your financial benefit! In the next chapter you will learn what commodity options contracts are.

Chapter 2

Introduction To Commodity Options

Now that we have covered futures contracts, you may be wondering what options are. When you visit investment or stock webpages, you will often see futures and options mentioned together. But what are options?

Options contracts are similar to futures contracts because they allow you to buy and sell options at a predetermined price. Unlike futures, however, you are under no obligation to purchase or sell these commodities even though you have the right. You can buy or sell these commodities at any time, although always within a specific period of time. With options contracts, you can purchase all sorts of commodities, including futures contracts, stocks and even property. (As stated at the beginning of this book, options contracts described in this book refer to agricultural options.)

Types of Options

There are two types of options: put options and call options. A put option gives you the right to sell your underlying commodity while a call option gives you the right to buy your underlying commodity. While both options types seem to be opposing sides of the same contract, this is not the case. A put option has a buyer and seller while a call option also has a buyer and a seller. In essence, both types of options contracts are very distinct, giving different rights to buyers and sellers.

Let's take an example. You want to purchase a piece of farmland, but do not want to purchase it immediately. Perhaps you do not have enough money or do not want to take on the responsibility just yet. You find a call option* to purchase a piece of land (80 acres) that meets your needs, with a price of $1,000 per acre. The owner of the land offers you a call option, giving you the right to purchase the land within three months. The price is locked in at $1,000 per acre during this time, giving you the right to purchase the land at that price, until the option expires in three months. To purchase the right to buy, you pay the option premium* of $17 per acre ($1,360). If you do not purchase the land before the option expires, you lose your right to buy. Alternatively, if your option contract states that your rights are transferable, you can resell your option contract at whatever price you choose - as long as it is before expiry.

On the other hand, if you want to sell your farmland, you will obtain a put option. You will then list the strike price* of the land before listing a call option to buyers. You have the right to sell to any of the buyers who approach you, ensuring that you do not break the terms of the options contract, for example by demanding more money than you formerly agreed to in the contract.

Options Premiums

Since options premiums are what are bought and sold in options contracts, the premium price is what often fluctuates the most. Just like with the futures industry, fluctuations in options premium prices depend on market conditions, including the time given until the contract expires, how volatile the market is at the time of sale/purchase, as well as other economic variables. Remember that options are derivative securities. This means that changes in

15

option prices are not the reflection of the option itself. Rather they are a reflection of the volatility* of the options market, as well as changes in the date of expiration and changes in the price of the underlying price. However, there is often a sense of financial stability with options, even despite the volatility of the market. Why? Because the underlying price plays a big part in the price of commodities, producing a quasi-stable investment market. This means that the price of peanuts would, most likely, not jump up 700% in one month, especially since supply of commodities to customers, businesses and investors is often global.

There are two parts of an option premium. These are the intrinsic value and the extrinsic value (time value).

Intrinsic Value

The intrinsic value of an option's contract is the tangible part of its price. Since options are sold with the potential promise of making the investor profits, the intrinsic value is, therefore, the options' built-in profit. It is calculated by finding the difference between the strike price and the underlying asset's price. A call option has intrinsic value if exercising the option will be profitable. In essence, an options contract has intrinsic value when you are able to buy it at a lower price than its current market price. If you want to purchase soybean futures in July with a strike price of $3.20 per bushel, the option only has intrinsic value if its underlying asset price is more than $3.20 per bushel. For example, if the underlying asset price is $3.50 per bushel at the time of your purchase and increases to $3.75 per bushel a few weeks later, its intrinsic value goes up from $0.30 to $0.55 per bushel. If the underlying asset price then reduces to $3.10 per bushel, it has no more intrinsic value.

A put option has intrinsic value if its strike price is higher than its underlying asset price. In this case, you are selling the options contract for more than its current market price. For example you want to sell your soybeans in July. The current market price is $3.40, but the strike price is $3.60. At this point, the option contract has intrinsic value for the seller because you are selling it for more than it is worth. If the strike price decreases to $3.30, then it has intrinsic value for the buyer who is buying for less than its market value.

For options that have no intrinsic value (because they would not make a profit if exercised) the premium is calculated based on the commodity's time value.

In the investment industry, an option that has intrinsic value is generally referred to as being "in-the-money." An option with no intrinsic value is referred to as being "out-of-the-money."

Extrinsic (Time) Value

The extrinsic value of an options contract represents its potential for making you profits. The buyer is always taking a risk when purchasing options, so an extrinsic value is baked into the contract that serves to allay your fears about the financial risks you are taking.

Extrinsic value, or time value, is the option's premium minus its intrinsic value. It reflects the amount of money that buyers are willing to pay for an option. The buyer invests, hoping that the option will make a profit at the time of exercising or before expiration. Time value of an options contract begins to decline once it is near expiration. By the time it reaches expiration, it will have no extrinsic value at all. The premium left on the contract post-expiration will be intrinsic value alone. Let's see an example. You want to purchase corn futures in May at the current price of $1.86. However, the strike price is currently at $2.00, then you would need to subtract $1.86 from $2.00 to find the extrinsic value, giving you $0.14.

If you want to exert the most extrinsic value from your trade, then purchase your options contract once it is at-the-money*. The moneyness* of options will let you know its intrinsic value, extrinsic value, time value and its potential volatility. Furthermore, the moneyness of options is very important for determining its time value. At-the-money options are the most likely options to move into the money before expiration. This is in contrast to in-the-money options whose monetary value are often eliminated before expiration. Why? In-the-money options have a greater likelihood and certainty of moving out of the money. The same is true of out-of-the money options. Likewise, your options will have a higher time value if you purchase them as early as possible. The less time an options contract has to expire, the lesser its time value will be. Options sellers typically sell their options for a higher price when expiration is far off because they are able to gamble that the option will be worth exercising (in the money) when/before expiration arrives. Options sellers are also sensitive to market volatility. The more variable* or volatile* the market, the more an options' time value increases since sellers demand a higher premium. This is because a more volatile or variable market increases the likelihood of the option being worth exercising (in-the-money). Essentially, the option moves more in a volatile market, since it is being traded more. This places pressure on whomever owns it to either sell or exercise, producing an in-the-money option. **Chapter Three** will discuss volatility in more depth.

Lastly, it should be noted that general interest rates also affect the time value of options. The high interest rates are, the more time value decreases.

Who Regulates Options?

Just like the futures market, the trading process of options premiums is also regulated by the exchange. In fact, the futures industry regulates the price and trading process of options premiums. Another similarity between options and futures contracts is the trading months of commodities. For example, the trading months for futures contracts of soybeans is June to September. The trading months for options contracts of soybeans is also June to September. As with futures, options trading also gives you the opportunity to trade during serial option months. Likewise, the serial option months* for futures contracts are also the same as options contracts.

No single person, business or regulatory body can set the price of commodities because they are traded on exchanges. That means that the price of commodities is simply determined by supply and demand. When there is less supply of oil, for instance, demand goes up. This, in turn, drives the price of a barrel of oil. Let's take another example. If there have been floods or civil unrest in a country that exports 40% of the world's peanuts, demand for peanuts worldwide will increase, despite reduced supply, causing the price of a bushel of peanuts to skyrocket. In fact, weather plays a big part in the fluctuations of price of commodities. While these are often short-term fluctuations, in recent years, climate change has also begun to affect long-term price changes. For example, if a wet climate suddenly begins to see less rainfall, it loses its optimal condition for food growth, causing prices of whatever commodity is grown in that climate to skyrocket.

Although the premium is not negotiated in the trading pit or regulated by anyone, other aspects of the options contract are. As with futures contracts, the CBOT standardizes and predetermines the expiration date, strike price and all other aspects of the options contract.

Purchasing Options Premiums

When looking at the commodity exchange, you will find that strike prices for each commodity are listed in multiples. These multiples are always predetermined based on underlying futures prices. In essence, the exchange will give you a range on the strike price based on the current underlying futures prices. However, it is still an exchange market, so strike prices for each agricultural commodity also decrease and increase according to the price of the commodity at the time. Since commodities also have typical trading months, there are always several options prices listed for different commodity options. Each price shows you the price of a particular contract month as well as the strike price. If you want to find the prices of commodities, check online exchange market sites. You can also check the Chicago Board Options Exchange (CBOE). Alternatively, you can also ask your broker for prices or check their website. Option prices are always listed on brokerage websites in what is called an "option chain*." An option chain presents you with all the available call and put options along with other important information, such as the exercise-by date, strike price, option price (also known as the option premium), and other data. Nowadays, there exist plenty of financial/investment apps that will also give you option prices. Speak with your broker about the best platform for checking option prices in your country/region, as each specific platform often has its advantages and disadvantages. You also have the added advantage of doing your own research to decide which source is best for you.

You can purchase premiums through your broker who pays the money to your options seller. Unlike with futures contracts, you do not need to maintain a margin account since you have to pay for the premium whether or not you choose to purchase the commodity(ies). Conversely, if you are selling options, you will need to post your margin with your broker since you are taking the risk by guaranteeing to sell your commodities to one buyer. The Chicago Board of Trade (CBOT) is very concerned with the risks sellers take. To regulate the market, they use a margin system called, SPAN. SPAN determines the overall risk of a potential commodity seller. In addition, it determines the required margin the seller will need to sell their commodities.

Opening An Account

Now that you know that you need to open an account with a reputable broker (usually a local brokerage office). Here are steps to teach you how to open an account.

1. Search for a local broker in your town or city. There will be one close to you. Try searching on your local government's website. You can also search for local grain elevator operators because some of them provide futures and options brokerage services.

2. Once you have found a list of brokers, check to see if the ones you choose are registered with the National Futures Association (NFA). According to US Federal Law, all brokers must be registered with the NFA. Federal law in the US requires that all brokers are registered with the NFA. You can contact the NFA by calling 0800 -621-3570.

3. If you are not in the US, there should be a regulatory body in your country that all brokers must register with. Said regulatory body will also have a list of all registered brokers.

4. If you are in the US, check with the NFA that no complaints have been registered with the broker you choose. If you are outside the US, check with the relevant regulatory body.

5. Do your own research. You are most often able to find websites of local commodity traders and investors. Once you do this try to contact current and past commodity traders and investors to ask them about their experience with local brokers. If you are able to find a list of current and past customers of the brokers you have chosen then contact them too for a more comprehensive and specific review and recommendation of your chosen brokers.

6. Once you choose your final brokerage firm and contact them about opening an account, they will send you an opening form. You will need to provide additional documentation such as your passport, your mortgage or rent payments or other utility bills. If

you are not a citizen of the country in which you reside, you will also need to provide proof of legal residency.

7. Once you open an account, you must inform your broker whether you plan to use your account for hedging or speculating. In some countries you will be provided a special investment/stockholder number that identifies only you and which will be used to trade in your name.

8. Once you begin to trade your broker will charge you a commission fee whether you want to buy or sell option contracts. Your commission rate will always vary depending on the brokerage firm and also the type and amount of service they offer. Don't let this put you off however because these rates are always competitive. So, if your broker is a fully service broker, s/he will be able to provide you a wider range of specialties and therefore may charge you more, depending on which specialties you demand. A discount broker who specialises only in executing trade, for example, may not charge as much as a fully service broker.

9. Be aware, however, that brokers often have special requirements when opening your account. For many brokers, your account will be considered inactive after a period of 6 months to 12 months without trade. For other brokers, your account may be cancelled after this period of 12 months.

10. Finally before you choose your broker, ensure that the one that you choose is specialized in the agricultural options market. If they are not specialized, they will not be able to advise you properly and may cost you money.

Pros and Cons of Options

There are many pros and cons to options contracts. They are:

Pros

- They are very diverse, allowing you to meet many of your trading or investment goals.
- With options, you have the right to buy, but are under no such obligation. With a lower financial commitment, you get to have your cake and eat it. If you decide to sell your options, you also get a lower financial commitment.
- Options offer you a more advanced investment option. This means you have more strategies for making a profit while mitigating risk. Since they are so diverse, they can be used by anyone to make a profit, regardless of your trading experience. There is always an options strategy out there for you to meet your investment goals.
- Options can be used as an asset for hedging your other investments. In fact, you can also use them to purchase other investments, such as stocks. In this sense, options work like money because you can use them to achieve your investment goals.
- Once you understand the rules of options trading, you can easily learn different strategies for making a profit.
- They bring a lot of stability to many different industries which, in turn, stabilize the economy. Let's take an example of how this works. An airline relies on a steady income stream to make its money and profit. To do this, it relies on the services and resources it uses being at a steady price. While it knows the estimated cost of paying all its human resources for the next year, it cannot calculate an estimated cost for fuel prices since fuel prices can suddenly increase or drop at any moment. This is especially pertinent since airlines have to purchase a large amount of gas. If an airline purchases gas only for prices to drop significantly the next day, it will have lost

hundreds of millions. Likewise, if prices increase 25% just before the airline purchases fuel, they also lose an extra 25% of their income. To protect itself financially from a volatile market, airlines purchase fuel in the options market at fixed rates, hedging the price of fuel to keep their fuel costs stable. By doing so, they protect themselves from significant financial loss which would also go on to affect local, national and even international economies.

Cons

- You can only buy options in increments of one or more contracts.
- With options trading, you can easily make a mistake or take the wrong step if you do not understand the complexities of options trading.
- No matter how good you are, you can never escape the possibility of making a loss, as with all investment options. Therefore, always follow the golden rule of investing: only invest what you are willing to lose.
- According to US law, you have to receive approval from your broker before you can begin trading options. Your broker will need to determine that you can trade options long-term before they will approve your application.

When Did Commodity Options Begin To Trade?

Commodities options can be traced all the way back to the beginning of civilization. In fact, the history of commodity trading can be found in its name: "trading." That is, the idea of commodity trading began with trading itself, when citizens within civilizations would trade one commodity for another. The farmer, for example, may trade his wheat for the weaver's fabric.

Indeed, commodity markets have been traced to the oldest civilization ever recorded, in Sumer, which was located in what is modern day Iraq. Between 4500 and 4000 BCE, citizens of Sumer would trade commodities (goats). This exchange was facilitated using the medium of clay tokens that were sealed in a clay vessel. Traders would decide the amount of goats to be purchased and sold during the exchange. Like commodity trading today, the exchange included contract details, including: the amount and price of commodities, the time of delivery and the date tells us that they were the earliest form of commodity futures contracts.

Sumer, of course, was not the only civilization that used commodity trading. As civilizations grew worldwide, they all had a form of commodity trading, since it is, essentially, the backbone of the economy. Other civilizations traded using all sorts of commodities, be it farm animals, seashells or any other common items used in place of money. These commodities, technically, served the purpose of "commodity money."

Today, of course, we have money. Although we take for granted the concept of money, the idea of trading commodities and money has changed over centuries. What started as the trading of agricultural commodities or other useful everyday items would eventually morph into the gold standard, when gold and silver became the commodity money driving the Commodities Exchange Market in classical civilizations.

The gold standard was an economic ideology which relied on a generally accepted value of gold. Just as today, we generally accept that money has intrinsic worth (because we all enter a social contract promising to honor its inherent worth). The popularity of silver and gold began, at first, because they were beautiful shiny, beautiful metals that never corroded. They could be melted and made into coins and other objects that retained their shine and beauty over many years, decades and centuries. They became a reliable medium of exchange used to pay for goods and commodities globally. As international trade developed, Britain and Paris soon became the centre of the gold standard. In the banks of London and Paris, the price of gold was set internationally. This gave traders more security in knowing that their gold and silver had a stable, standard price for their commodities. This, in turn, drove trades as well as drove the normalization of the commodities trading of gold and silver. Countries that opted into the gold standard would have to ensure that they had enough gold and silver to back up their Commodities Trading Exchange and, as a direct consequence, their economy. Without enough gold or silver reserves, traders would be unwilling to trade in a country because they could not be assured of receiving the standard price at the time for their goods and commodities. This means that they could be used to trade for items while retaining their value. This is also how the international currency exchange began, since world banks (in Paris and London) monitored and set regular prices of gold and silver to ensure market stability.

As a result, gold merged into one of global civilization's first forms of commodity trading.

In mediaeval Europe, commodity markets slowly morphed as traders travelled internationally by ships and boats. Merchants preferred to accept gold in exchange for their commodities. Commodities trading was a reliable way for merchants to distribute land, goods, labor, and capital across Western Europe. Outside Europe, gold would also be used as a medium of commodities exchange.

Soon, regions began making their own forms of coin using gold and silver, with the value of gold and silver based on weight. By the 1500s, the gold and silver was used so extensively worldwide that stock exchanges began to emerge to manage the exchange of these coins.

In 1530, the world's first stock exchange was created, however, it was originally created as a commodity exchange market. It allowed traders to buy and sell options, short sales and forward contracts. Over the next two centuries, other commodity exchange markets were opened in other cities in Europe. By 1864, the CBOT (Chicago Board of Trade) opened, trading cattles, pigs, corn and wheat. By the 1930s, the CBOT expanded its commodity exchange to include potatoes, mill feeds, eggs, rice, butter, soybeans, and potatoes. Although the CBOT is known as the world's oldest futures and options exchange market, the Amsterdam Stock Exchange is considered to be the first by some economists.

In medieval Europe people struggled to determine the value of units of commodities. That is, how much should a bushel of potatoes or a bullion of gold weigh, for example. This was one of many determining rules of options trading that had to reach a consensus between all stakeholders. There also needed to be consensus on the quality and definition of each commodity.

As commodity exchange markets developed, stakeholders, such as banks, governments and the different boards of trade, began to regulate the industry. In 1934, the US government created the Commodity Price Index to chart and index 22 basic commodities that were most sensitive to and influenced by changes in economic conditions. This model of commodity price indexes* is still used today by most countries worldwide. In the United States, this index is published as part of the Producer Price Index (PPI) by the American Bureau of Labor Statistics. The ProducerPrice Index has a commodities list of over 3,500 items.

Futures and Commodity Options Markets Around The World

Here are some futures and options markets around the developed world, although not all of them trade in agricultural commodities:

- Chicago Mercantile Exchange (CME).

Trades in livestock, energy, financials, precious metals and industrial metals commodities.

- Chicago Board of Trade (CBOT).

Trades in livestock and agricultural commodities.

- Korea Exchange (KRS).

Trades in precious metals and financial commodities.

- New York Board of Trade (NYBOY).

Trades in agricultural commodities.

- New York Mercantile Exchange (NYMEX).

Trades in precious metals and energy commodities.

- Australian Stock Exchange (ASE).

Trades in agricultural, financial, energy, and environmental commodities.

- London Metal Exchange (LME).

Trades in industrial metal commodities.

- Brazilian Mercantile and Futures Exchange (BM&F).

Trades in financial and agricultural commodities.

- Tokyo Commodities Exchange (TOCOM).

Trades in industrial metals, energy, rubber and precious metals commodities.

- NYSE Euronext (ASE).

Based in France and trades in agricultural, energy, financial and environmental commodities.

This is a list of the most popular futures and commodities markets in the developed world. However, there are futures and options markets all over the world devoted to only agricultural commodities. In many cases, these niche markets sell just one or two agricultural commodities, such as the Minneapolis Grain Exchange (MGEX). Furthermore, there are plenty of options trading markets in the developing world, such as the Africa Exchange (AFEX), the East African PanXchange Physical Commodities Market and the National Commodity & Derivative Exchange (NCDEX) in India, which trades agricultural commodities, as well as gold.

Chapter Summary

- Options contracts are similar to futures contracts because they allow you to buy and sell options at a predetermined price.
- With options contracts, you are under no obligation to purchase or sell these commodities even though you have the right.

- With options contracts, you can purchase all sorts of commodities, including futures contracts, stocks and even property.
- Changes in option prices are not the reflection of the option itself. They are a reflection of the volatility of the options market. They also reflect the date of expiration and changes in the price of the underlying asset.
- There are two types of options: put options and call options.
- Since options premiums are what are bought and sold in options contracts, the premium price is what often fluctuates the most.
- Fluctuations in premium prices depend on market conditions.
- The intrinsic value of an options premium is the difference between its strike price and the underlying asset's price.
- Extrinsic value, or time value, is the option's premium minus its intrinsic value. It reflects the amount of money that buyers are willing to pay for an option
- The price of commodities is simply determined by supply and demand. It is not regulated by a single body.
- The price of commodities is determined by supply and demand.
- Strike prices for each agricultural commodity decrease and increase according to the price of the commodity at the time.
- The CBOT standardizes the expiration date, strike price and all other aspects of the options contract.
- Option prices are always listed on brokerage websites in what is called an "option chain."
- With options, you do not need to maintain a margin account since you have to pay for the premium whether or not you choose to purchase the commodity.

- When selling options, you will need to post your margin with your broker since you are taking a risk by guaranteeing to sell your commodities to just one buyer.
- Commodities options can be traced all the way back to the beginning of civilization.
- As civilizations grew worldwide, they all had a form of commodity trading.
- What originally began as the trading of agricultural commodities, or other useful everyday items, would eventually morph into the gold standard, when gold and silver became the medium, or commodity money, driving the Commodities Exchange Market in classical civilizations.
- Gold is one of global civilization's first forms of commodity trading.

In the next chapter you will learn whether commodity options trading is profitable.

Chapter 3

Is Commodity Options Trading Profitable?

Before we can determine whether commodity options trading is profitable, we must first understand how exactly it is used in business, or, how it is used to make a profit. As already briefly discussed there are a few stakeholders in options trading. All these stakeholders hope to make a profit from the options market, albeit in different ways. Farmers use the options market to lock in a profitable selling price for their crops. Failing that, they understand that they can use it to obtain a "price insurance" when they store their crops. In essence, options trading is a price/selling guarantee for farmers, protecting them from the whims and ups and downs of the market.

If you work in the food manufacturing and processing industry, you will be very interested in options trading. Businesses and individuals in the agribusiness sector of processing and manufacturing are very interested in trading (buying) agricultural commodities. Why? Because they have a chance to purchase much-needed commodities at a lower price. Agricultural commodities are the backbone of their business but, as you can imagine, purchasing thousands, tens of thousands, hundreds of thousands and even millions of bushels worth of commodities per year can get very expensive if purchased from a market with regulated prices. For example, if a food manufacturing plant uses corn to produce cereal, they may purchase a put option, anticipating a drop in corn prices in a few months and hoping to capitalise on that. Options trading gives them the ability to improve their profitability over the long time. It also gives them the opportunity to protect the value of their on hand inventory. How do they do this? By "manipulating the market" through options trading.

If the price of corn options reduces significantly because of a new hardy variety of corn, for example, customers will begin to demand lower cereal prices. In this case, the company's on hand cereal inventory will see a sharp decline in value and profits. To prevent this from occurring, the food manufacturer might decide to increase the perceived scarcity of corn on the market. If the price of corn options begins to climb too high, the agribusiness may decide to purchase put options and then hold until they can buy for a very low price. That way they can buy as much of the corn on the market as possible to hoard it, thereby creating a fake scarcity and causing the price of corn options to climb back up.

Furthermore, elevator operators are another heavy stakeholder in options trading. They typically offer their customers marketing offers paid out in agricultural options, such as minimum price contract offers which allows food producers and farmers to set up a minimum price for their crop with the flexibility of increasing their final sale price at expiration. With these offers, elevator operators hope to keep their existing clients as well as attract new ones, giving them a competitive edge.

Just like farmers, feedlot managers* use the options market as a way to protect themselves from the fluctuations of the exchange, especially when fluctuations mean that grain prices, for example, increase significantly.

Of course, bankers and brokers are very interested in the options exchange market. It is, after all, a market exchange, where money is made and profit and losses are recorded daily. The broker and the banker are both very invested in the market because they represent and manage other stakeholders. If the exchange market itself does well, so, too, they do well. Likewise, the more regulated the market is, the more motivated stakeholders are in trading in that particular market. Brokers and bankers have a lot of influence in ensuring that the options market is well regulated and stable - to an extent.

Finally, the last stakeholder that is motivated primarily by profit is the investor. The investor tries to find the best method, and the most risk averse way to make the most amount of profit. What can definitely be argued is that the actions and motivations of individual stakeholders in the options exchange market, keeps the market alive. Each stakeholder, primarily motivated to make a profit, inadvertently fuels the market and fuels the desires for profit of the other stakeholders. Therefore, the market itself has become a self-contained, self-reliant one.

In this chapter, we will uncover the different ways in which options trading can result in profit for you, the beginner investor.

Volatility

Volatility is very important because it impacts the price of options, just as volatility impacts every other market. Volatility tells you how market prices are fluctuating. In the options market, volatility tells you how market prices of the underlying futures are fluctuating. A high volatility means more frequent and more rapidly swaying price fluctuations, while a low volatility means the opposite.

The price of options is determined based on how likely the underlying futures are to finish in-the-money (ITM) or, at the very least, with some intrinsic value. With more likelihood to finish with intrinsic value or ITM, the options contract becomes more expensive.

Of course, to determine the likelihood of an asset finishing profitably, stakeholders consider several factors, including how much time the option has until it expires, the price of the asset and how likely the option is to expire profitably, based on external influences. For example, a sudden increase in demand for corn indicates that corn options are more likely to expire profitably in the next couple of months.

Conversely, an option's volatility is also determined by its price. Cheaper options have less volatility because they are more likely to be bought and sold on the market, causing the option to become in-the-money. On the other hand, the more an options' volatility increases, the more the prices of any options on that underlying asset increase too - whether call or put options. This increase occurs because the likelihood of all options on that underlying asset finishing in the money also increases.

There are two types of volatility that help you understand how options work: implied volatility and historic volatility (HV).

Implied Volatility

Unlike historic volatility, implied volatility is a way of estimating option prices in real time. Think of implied volatility as a financial metric for calculating/predicting the likelihood of changes/fluctuations in a given option's price. As an investor, implied volatility is a great metric to help you predict which options will most likely be profitable and which ones won't. In essence, you can be more successful trading options if you use implied volatility as a metric to calculate what underlying assets to invest in and the best time to invest in them. Additionally, this metric helps you project how much supply and demand an underlying asset will see and how that is likely to affect options prices.

Usually, implied volatility will increase when the options market sees a downtrend because options are seeing less trade and less

35

movement between owners. With less trade in the options market, volatility increases as price stability decreases. Consequently, with a downtrend in the market, stakeholders feel more pressure to buy and sell, but also to hold, causing stark fluctuations on the market and higher option prices. Conversely, IV also falls when the options market sees an increase in popularity. With more stakeholders buying and selling, there is an increased stability in the market. This stability naturally reduces volatility.

Implied volatility also affects the strike price of options. An option with a strike price near the money is very sensitive due to implied volatility. An option with a strike price at the money or out of the money is less sensitive to changes due to implied volatility. An option's premium consists of extrinsic and/or intrinsic value. When we're talking implied volatility, we are focusing only on the extrinsic value of an options price.

You could say that IV illustrates how much extrinsic value a stock option has in relation to the time until its expiration date. Hence, IV is simply the extrinsic value of a stock option relative to the time until its expiration. With implied volatility, you can predict the expected move of an option. What do I mean by expected move?

The "expected move" of any financial security is how much a stock is expected/predicted to fall or rise from its current market price. The expected move is based on the security's current level of implied volatility. Your stock option's expected move can either be one standard deviation, two standard deviation or three. Standard deviation is the expected probability that a stock's price will fall or rise in the future. Or, to put it differently, standard deviation predicts the magnitude of your options price movement with a certain percentage of certainty. A one standard deviation range typically encompasses 68.2% of expected outcomes, while a two standard deviation range typically encompasses 95.4%. Lastly, a three standard deviation encompasses 99.7%.

Standard deviation is used to calculate expected move because the price of underlying assets is always going either up or down on the market - usually moving up or down in the same direction for consecutive days. Standard deviation is simply a response to regular market movements. 68.2% of the time, stock price movements go up or down for 1-3 consecutive days. It becomes rarer, climbing up to 4-7 days of consecutive rise or fall 95.4% of the time and 7+ days of consecutive rise or fall 99.7% of the time. Less likely to occur standard deviations are known as black swans*.

Example:

Let's take a good example. Your soybean options are currently worth $2.50 a bushel. Your implied volatility is 50% and your 1 SD (one standard deviation) is $1.75 to $4.00. That means that there is a 68.2% probability (1 SD) that your soybean stock options will stay within +50% or -50% of its current price of $2 50 within one year. It is certainly possible for the stock price to go below or above this price range, but the probability of this occurring is relatively low.

If your underlying asset has a low implied volatility, then you can predict that it will very likely not move either upwards or downwards in price from its current stock price over the next 12 months (or until its expiration date). While the steady market prices that low implied volatility brings are clear benefits, you also have the advantage of less likelihood of loss - but also less likelihood of profits. With high implied volatility, there are wild swings in market prices over the next 12 months (or until its expiration date), with a higher likelihood of making both a loss and a profit.

A bearish market* (prices of underlying assets decreasing over a period of time) most often leads to high implied volatility. Sellers of options contracts benefit most from a bearish market. A <u>bullish market*</u> (prices of underlying assets increasing over a period of time) conversely most often leads to low implied volatility. Buyers of options contracts benefit most from a bearish market. If your investment strategy is in the long-term bullish market, a bearish market increases your risk of significant loss. Likewise, if your investment strategy is in the long-term bearish market, a bullish market increases your risk of significant loss. Sooner or later, high implied volatility trends fall. As a result, option traders like you prefer to sell their call and put options during times of high implied volatility and buy both call and put options during times of low implied volatility.

You can usually find out the implied volatility of your option from your broker or on the option chain of your broker platform. However, if the implied volatility of your options is not available to you, you can calculate it yourself using the Black-Scholes Model (BSM) or the Binomial Model. (I would advise, however, that this is a very advanced technique that should only be used once you have mastered commodity options trading.)

Stock options have multiple implied volatilities, each based on respective expiration cycles. When checking the implied volatility of your stock options, use the implied volatility of the options with the expiration cycle closest to your own expiration cycle. As an example, when checking the option chain on your stock, you may see that it has four expiration cycles: three months, six months, nine months and a year. If your stock options expire in seven months, then your implied volatility is the six months option.

Just like any other market, to make money from options trading, you need to keep a constant watch on the market itself. Market trends are your key to whether options trading is profitable for you or not. In fact, this is a key difference between options trading and stock trading. With stock trading, you may decide to ignore or neglect your stocks for a short-term or long-term period and simply allow the market to do what it wants. However, with options trading, since it uses a shorter-term when trading, every single trend in the market is likely to affect your option prices. As a result you need to keep a very close eye on the market, as well as on stock market announcements and major news events. Essentially, options trading requires that you be financially and politically in-the-know.

What this means is that, if you are not a politically or financially literate person, you will most likely make a loss when trading options. You need to be able to understand the political and financial ramifications of major new stories and world events so that you can understand how they will affect any option contracts that you possess.

The more financially and politically literate you are, the more likely you are to also decipher some of the more intricate ways in which major news events will affect your options. That is, the more deep knowledge you possess concerning politics and economy, the more likely you are to make a profit off of your options.

As a beginner, one of the best ways to begin to develop your knowledge is to simply throw yourself into it. Read major news stories everyday and predict how you think this will affect your options. You don't necessarily have to use these stories to decide on whether to buy stock options. You can simply predict how you think these news stories will affect options and then watch to see whether you are right or wrong.

Even the simplest market changes will cause implied volatility to either increase or decrease. If you want your options to yield higher premiums then pay attention to the implied volatility of your options. For example, you could decide to wait until news of a merger or profits are about to be announced. Depending on whether you want to buy or sell, this could either mean a profit or loss for you. You can see, then, how this is a good strategy for predicting option prices to your benefit.

Conversely, there are disadvantages to using implied volatility as a metric for predicting changes in securities' prices. For one, IV based entirely on market prices, ignoring fundamentals* in the process. This same disadvantage also applies to sudden and unexpected events. Implied volatility relies on economic and political stability. It does not take into account how unexpected events will affect the market. Lastly, as already discussed, IV is great for predicting the possibility of movement, but fails to disclose whether this movement is a profit or loss.

Historical Volatility

Also known as statistical volatility or realized volatility, historical volatility is a metric used to measure past market fluctuations. It offers a quantitative way to understand how underlying securities perform on the market by analysing price change fluctuations over a period of time. Although it can be used to predict the future, just as IV does, historic volatility does so by analysing past data to find possible patterns that can then be used to predict future market fluctuations.

The goal with historical volatility is to learn from the past. As you can imagine, using past experiences to predict present and future market changes is a common financial tactic. Nonetheless, it is a less popular metric than implied volatility because it requires more effort and financial and mathematical know-how to gather financial data from the past, analyse it coherently and then make predictions based on this information. Another reason for IV's greater popularity is because financial markets are always evolving, so investors feel less confident basing their investment decisions on simple past fluctuations. As you will see later in this chapter, hower, past fluctuations can still be put to good use in more sophisticated ways to determine whether to invest in stock options or not.

Just like implied volatility, a rise in historical volatility causes more fluctuations in the price of securities. A lower HV, on the other hand, reduces uncertainty among investors, bringing stability to market prices, as well as the trade of securities.

Typically, historical volatility is calculated based on intraday* changes or increments between one closing price and the subsequent day's closing price. Increments can be larger too, going up to 180 days. As you can imagine, the longer the increment (or period of time) being compared, the more data investors have. Subsequently, the more data, the more extensive, information-rich and reliable your findings.

Imagine the calculated average historical volatility of corn futures over the past 180 days is 15%. The calculated implied volatility of the same security is 32%. As an investor, both figures tell you that corn is trading at a higher volatility than its average over the last six months. If you are a bearish investor, this may be a good time to sell.

You can check the historical volatility of underlying assets on your trading platform, or by contacting your broker.

Volatility Skew

As well as implied volatility and historical volatility, there is also volatility skew. While volatility skew is more of an advanced concept, you should still know the basics as a beginner options trader. So how does volatility skew work?

Although an underlying asset can have just one volatility, this does not translate to every option contract on the same underlying asset. So, the volatility of wheat will not necessarily be the same across different options contracts. This happens because the same option will trade at different implied volatilities, depending on their strike prices and expiration date. So, the put option of wheat will likely have a lower volatility than the call option of wheat because put options provide loss protection and, therefore, usually have lower volatility. This is what is meant by being "skewed".

Your job as a trader is to figure out whether your options contract is skewed towards high or low volatility. You can do this by checking its risk profile file on your brokerage platform. If your contract is skewed towards high volatility, you can also attempt to balance it out and reduce volatility risk by hedging one contract against another.

From what you have learnt on volatility in this chapter, it is most certain that volatility is a very important factor in understanding and deciding whether or not an options contract will be profitable for you. Stakeholders in the options market use both implied volatility and historical volatility to predict market movements. In fact, both these metrics, used together, directly influence options prices. One major way in which they influence options price is through time value, which sees great degrees of fluctuation based on volatility. As a trader, it is in your best interest to use both implied and historical volatility. Clearly, combining the data from both metrics will give you more reliable information. This method is also more reliable because it combines both a past-measuring and forward-looking metric to predict underlying security prices.

The best way to approach historical and implied volatility is to think of both as sharing an interdependent relationship. To better understand one, you must fully understand the other. At the same time, historical volatility acts as a sort of root for options metrics. Its quantitative data results are more stable than the more fluctuating, predicted results of implied volatility.

As an investor/options trader, you cannot afford not to pay attention to volatility. Why? Well, during periods of high IV and HV, you will obviously benefit as an options seller (or a bearish investor). During periods of low IV and HV, you will obviously benefit as an options buyer (or a bullish investor). What's more, the volatility of options will enlighten you on what hedging tactics you can use to get the most out of your contract. Essentially, deviations stable IV and HV is your cue to take advantage of either undervalued or overvalued options premiums

You will have heard the mantra: "Buy low. Sell high". By keeping abreast of fluctuations in volatility, you can do so. Hence, if you have options premiums that you want to sell, then you will need to look for spikes in implied volatility, i.e. periods when implied volatility is higher than average. Your options premiums will be overvalued and you can make significant profit from selling it at inflated premiums. You have the advantage in that market and can close your position at a profit before volatility stabilizes once more.

As a buyer, you can still sell high and buy low by using the same strategy and looking for dips in implied volatility, i.e. periods when implied volatility is lower than average. Options premiums will be undervalued and you can make significant profit from buying low and later selling high at inflated premiums.

Notwithstanding the HV or IV, timing is still key for making good trades. Yes, implied and historical volatility will significantly reduce your chances of a bad trade, but trading at just the perfect time is one unpredictable part of the financial market for which no mathematical formula has still been found. You must, consequently, embrace the idea that, as with all things in life, there will always be risks with options trading. For good measure, even if you make the perfect market call at the perfect time, you could still end up losing money if wide price swings trigger a margin call* or stop-loss* on your account.

Implied Volatility Rank

Another wonderful way to use the relationship between historical and implied volatility to your benefit is the implied volatility rank. If you have some experience in options trading, you may be wondering why you have never heard of this term. The implied volatility rank (commonly referred to as IV rank, compares current IV levels to the maximum and minimum historical IV levels over a 52-week period. You can deduce from this information that, by using the IV rank, we get insights into whether present-day options are cheaper or more expensive than normal on a relative basis. Even better, the IV rank allows you to rank/measure whether the implied volatility of an underlying asset is high or low relative to, not just its level in the past, but also relative to other options.

Yes, knowing the implied volatility of an option is very important, as we have explored in this chapter. Still, you can never have too much knowledge. The IV rank came about as a way to build upon the information that the implied volatility brings you so that you can make even more informed trading choices. Hence, with the IV rank, you can measure whether an option may be overpriced or underpriced relatively speaking.

How does it work? You take a stock option's current implied volatility and compare it against the historic range of implied volatilities for that same option. Its value will determine where it is ranked between the minimum rank, 0 and the maximum rank, 100. Based on where that stock option is ranked, you will know how high or low the option's current IV measures compared to where it has ranked at different times in the past 52 weeks.

Example:

You have six rankings for IV at: 10, 12, 17, 21, 25 and 31. The current IV for the commodity option you want to purchase is 10. Hence, its IV rank would be 0 because it is ranked at the lowest level in the range. If it was 21, the IV rank would be 50 since it is right in the middle of the range. Lastly, if it was 31, its IV rank would be 100, as it is at the highest level in the range.

As we've established, using implied volatility alone to decide whether to invest in options can be misleading. As an example, the implied volatility of beans stock options is at 15%. This might seem like a great time to invest (i.e. buy low, sell high) until you measure the IV rank, which tells you beans stock options at the current price is ranked at 85, showing that beans stock options prices have been much lower in the past.

Naturally, most investors use both IV and IV rank to get a fuller picture of a stock's volatility. Concurrently, IV rank can sometimes oversimplify your choice. You do want to buy low, but IV rank often does not take into consideration other factors affecting the price of options. Beans option prices might have an IV rank of 0, so you might be tempted to buy some with the plan to sell high, but the IV rank does not tell you why it is low. Perhaps external factors, such as harvest surplus, will mean that you won't be able to sell high even if you buy low.

Similarly, watch out for earning announcements. In general, earning announcements cause huge spikes in both implied volatility and implied volatility rank. As you can imagine, this is caused by the uncertainty of the market at this time. Always research earning announcements of companies that are associated with the option you want to purchase before purchase. If an earning announcement is upcoming, you might want to wait until the market stabilizes before making an investment.

Moreover, don't fall into the trap most beginners fall into, thinking that IV and IV rank will work perfectly every time. IV rank of underlying assets will often stay low or high for a long time - sometimes for weeks and months. It is in your best interest to use IV and IV rank as part of a comprehensive strategy, and one of many deciding factors for making market plays. For good measure, always keep in mind that there is never any certainty when making investments!

Implied Volatility Percentile

IV rank can be expressed as a percentile. When this happens, it is called an implied volatility percentile. Just like IV rank, this percentile ranges from 0 to 100, although in percentage.

When you read investment blogs, financial newspapers, and so on, you will often see the IV percentile used as a metric for deciding whether a stock is ripe for investment. The IV percentile is one of the most common metrics used for measuring and ranking stock prices because it is mean-reverting*. This simply means that low implied volatility and high implied volatility cannot stay that way forever. What goes up eventually comes down and what goes down eventually comes back up. Or, in other words, stock option prices are not stuck in a perpetual state of consistency. If they were, we would not need implied volatility in the first place. The market is also made up of traders who are not able to withstand constant wild swings in perpetuity. Traders and investors are people. No matter how logical you try to approach investments, you cannot divorce your emotions from the process. Too much volatility causes traders to live in a state of constant fear, so volatility will always revert back to stable after a while.

As described above, IV and UV rank/percentile are best used as part of a comprehensive strategy, and one of many deciding factors for making market plays. Other deciding factors include:

- Realized volatility.

Implied volatility is implied. It is what the market thinks, believes and predicts will happen in the future. It is often not the same as realized volatility, which is actually what happens.

What actually happens (realized volatility) is what will determine whether or not your options make a profit or loss. For example, if your options have a 95% IV percentile and an IV of 150%, you

46

may be tempted to think you need to take this window of opportunity to sell high and make a profit.

Once you sell, the implied volatility could climb higher. This means that you make less profit than if you had held or you make a loss if the realized volatility in this case suddenly swings to a loss

- Earning announcements and other announcements.

Earnings and other announcements regularly cause stocks with a high IV rank to have a low realized volatility. To avoid this high volatility and subsequent crash post-announcement, investors will sell their stock options before big announcements.

- Seasons.

Agricultural commodities are notorious for being affected by the seasons. Unlike company stocks, agricultural commodities are, in most cases, produced because of the seasons. Food agricultural commodities completely depend on harvest for their existence, for example.

For example, the implied volatility of corn commodities will certainly see a decrease after an announcement that global corn production for the year has been a recorded surplus.

Similarly, the IV rank of wheat commodities will increase after an announcement that wheat has not been sown as usual this year because of a fertilizer crisis. Even non-food agricultural commodities, such as petroleum, see their implied volatility affected greatly by seasonal changes as well as any other unexpected changes.

The implied volatility of natural gas will see an increase during winter months because more people need/rely on natural gas to heat their homes, bringing more uncertainty if supply and demand to the market. At the same time, if a country that is dependent on natural gas during the winter decides to invest in other sources of energy, for example, solar panels or nuclear power, then implied volatility of natural gas will see a spike because traders are worried that this non-seasonal change will decrease demand for their commodity.

As a beginner trader, you will make some errors as you learn what works best for you. That is why I recommend you start slow and then build up your trade confidence. There are some things that seem like "common sense" investment decisions, but can end up being mistakes. One such common mistake is thinking that if the IV percentile or rank is at its highest, the implied volatility will be unable to go higher too. Rather, it just means the measure for determining the IV percentile or rank gets a wider range. In a sense, this is a disadvantage of the IV percentile/rank system because the percentile/rank will continue to stay at 100 no matter how much the IV rises, thereby increasing your chances of making a loss on your investments. I cannot, therefore, stress the importance of not using just the implied volatility and its accompanying measures as your only measure for making buy/sell decisions. In fact, investors argue on whether or not the IV and IV rank/percentile systems are any good when used as a sole measure for making market calls.

As well as implied volatility, you can also measure an option's ever-changing value according to changes in its underlying price, time and interest rates. These metrics are known as Greeks. As a beginner trader, I would recommend that you learn about the Greeks once you move to an advanced level of trading knowledge and experience.

Speculating and Hedging Options

Options contracts (both calls and puts) are mainly used by investors to hedge against risks in their already existing investments. So, if you are an options investor who trades in stock and owns stocks, you may decide to buy or sell options as a way to hedge your direct investment in the underlying asset. Essentially options are often used as a secondary way of making money for investors because they can be a very profitable form of investing. Some investors use options as a secondary form of making money to partially compensate for any possible losses that they incur from their underlying asset.

Likewise, not every investor uses options as a supplementary or compensatory investment form. Speculative traders like to use options as a standalone investment in commodity markets. Speculative trading in the options and futures commodity market is very popular because it offers speculators an advantage they often don't get in other exchange markets: a high level of leverage.

Speculative traders and the options commodity market have a mutually beneficial relationship. Since the commodity market is not as popular an exchange market as the stock exchange, there are less traders and, therefore, less liquidity. Speculative traders improve market participation and liquidity. Consequently, they reduce volatility because of this increase in liquidity and market participation. In fact, the options market sees more trades driven by speculators. I.e., the more speculators trade, the more long haul options' investors trade, worried about commodity shortages and not being able to make a profit from the market.

Furthermore, speculators stabilize the market, thereby making it more profitable. By increasing market participation, there are too many traders holding too many trading positions. As a result, there are too many market participants for even the largest holders in the market to attempt too many successful market manipulations. Without any one trader or group of traders trying to corner the market, options trading sees more stability, increasing the conditions needed for profitability.

Making Profits From Commodity Trading Examples

As a beginner, you may be struggling with how to put the concepts described in this chapter (and in this book) into practice. So, here are a few examples of the different strategies you can take to make a profit from commodity trading.

Example 1: **Buying a Put Option To Minimize Loss**

As already discussed, put options are a great way to minimize the risk of loss. Usually investors or stakeholders in the commodity market purchase put options when prices are falling because it is a way to ensure that you can still set the minimum price or strike price for your particular commodity without losing profitability. It is also a great way to buy low and eventually sell high. Let's see an example.

You are a new investor without much capital, seeking to begin trading in the commodities market. Prices of commodities are generally high at the moment, but you notice that the strike prices of soybeans are unusually low. After some research, you find out that there has been an over-production of soybeans globally, causing supply to exceed demand. You decide that soybeans will climb up in price in a few months once supply stabilizes, so you invest in soybeans by purchasing put options. You speak to a soybean farmer who assures you that soybean planting just finished and there won't be as much soybeans produced the next harvest because farmers don't feel it is profitable enough. Farmers are also worried that prices will continue to plunge before harvest, resulting in record losses, so they are happy to sell low now to reduce threats to their profitability.

Based on your research and the market, you purchase put options for November soybeans at a strike price of $6.00 per bushel. You now have to sell your soybeans at a minimum selling price of $6.00 per bushel (minus commissions and the option cost). A week before harvest, November soybean futures price is now at $5.00, meaning your options are now in-the-money. You now have two choices:

Example 2: **Buying a Put Option to Protect Your Investments**

A put option is always a great way to minimize your risk of loss. You can buy put options to set a minimum selling price while keeping your ability to profit from higher prices. This is an especially good strategy to use when commodity prices are falling.

Imagine you are a pig farmer, who sells frozen pork bellies i.e. bacon. The pork industry is notorious for wild price swings, so buying put options is one way in which you ensure that you are in control of the minimum selling price of your product while, at the same time, retaining the opportunity to take advantage of and profit from higher prices.

Your pigs will be ready for slaughter in six months. You are anxious that prices of pork will drop before this time. To set a floor price for your expected pork harvest, you decide to purchase April frozen pork bellies put with a strike price of $4.00 per pound. Your minimum selling price for frozen pork bellies is $4.00 excluding commissions, the cost of the option and basis).

By March, April options price falls to $3.75, putting your put option in the money. You decide to exercise your option, thereby receiving a short options contract at the $4.00 strike price. If you buy back the contract at $3.75 a pound, you get a profit of $0.25 per pound (calculated by subtracting the difference between the options' price and the strike price). This difference should roughly offset the lower price of pork.

On the other hand, rather than the exercising the option, you can decide to sell it back to someone else, hedging that you would make more profit this way. If you decide to sell, you will profit from the remaining time value and the $0.25 intrinsic value, as will be presented in the option premium

Once April soybeans begin trading at $3.75, your pork put option will then be worth $0.25 combined with the remaining time value. You may decide to then offset (i.e. sell) the option rather than exercising it. Exercising the option will give you only its intrinsic value. As a farmer, you need all the income you can get. This means that you may also not be willing to pay your broker the extra commission charged for exercising the option.

Conversely, if the price of pork increases just before your contract reaches expiration and is still above the option strike price, your put is out of the money. You can let the option expire in that case, or you can choose to sell it back before expiration to try to regain the time value at the very least.

Whether you choose to exercise or allow it to expire, you won't lose anymore the premium you paid. Yet, you will still have the option to sell your pork at a higher price.

Example 3: **Buying a Call Option To Minimize Threats To Your Profitability**

As has already been briefly discussed with the airline example, many manufacturers, companies, and so on, rely on options to minimize threats to their profitability. Art and price fluctuations can make it difficult for companies to plan their financial future. Options are a great way for companies to gain a sense of financial stability, giving them the freedom to plan ahead financially and to retain market presence and gain market value.

Whether you are a big company or a small company, trading options is always a great way to ensure that you can continue to manufacture your products at a consistent price. As a result, even customers rely on options trading. That is, customers reliant on consistent prices depend on businesses and manufacturers themselves to purchase options as a way to minimize serious fluctuations in price.

Another advantage is that, although rising commodity prices are a threat to company profitability, buying call options still allows companies to establish a maximum purchase price without giving up the opportunity to profit from falling prices. Let's take an example.

You run a small cereal manufacturing plant and need to purchase oats in May. Thanks to increased demand for cereal globally, you are worried that prices will rise in the next few months. To prevent having to minimize threats to your profitability, you decide to set a ceiling price for your eventual purchase. You purchase a May oats call with a 20 cent strike price. Consequently, you then have a maximum purchase price of 20 cents a bushel (excluding the cost of the option, basis and commissions).

In April, if the May futures price rises to 25 cents your call option is now in the money. This means you can exercise your option, thereby receiving a long futures contract at the 20 cent strike price. You can then sell back the futures contract at the higher market price (25 cents per pound) gives you a 5-cent profit, per bushel. This 5-cent profit would offset the increase in the cost of oats.

Similarly, rather than choosing to exercise the option, you could earn even more profit by offsetting the option position, i.e selling the option (see **Chapter Six**). By doing this, you are able to profit from both the remaining time value and the increase in intrinsic value. Both of these would then be reflected in the option premium.

The 20-cent oats call would still be worth any remaining time value as well as its intrinsic value of 5 cents at the very least (remembering that the intrinsic value is the difference between the strike price and the option price).

If the price of oats falls in April below the option's strike price, your call option is then is out of the money. You can then let your option expire. Alternatively, you can sell your option back before expiration. This way, you won't lose more than the premium you paid and still have the option to purchase however much bushels of oats you purchased at the lower market price.

Example 4: **Selling Options to Make a Profit**

As an option seller, you get your full premium back from whomever buys your option from you. As ever, the option comes with obligation, meaning that you are legally obliged to sell to the buyer if they decide to exercise their options.

If the option seller exercises their call, you get a short position at the strike price while the buyer gets a long futures position at the same strike price. On the other hand, if a put option is exercised, it works in reverse. You get a long futures position at the option strike price while the buyer gets a short futures position at the same strike price.

Let's take an example. You invested in some wheat options hoping to make a person profit in a few months. You soon realise that December wheat prices will very likely fall or stay the same. To make a profit, you sell a wheat call for December at a strike price of $4.10 for 10 cents a bushel, giving you a maximum profit of 10 cents per bushel (minus commissions).

By October, you notice the December wheat future price goes down to $4.00, meaning that your call option is out-of-the-money. To offset your position, you can buy back the call option at $4.00 even though its remaining time value is at 5 cents a bushel. In this scenario, you make a profit of 5 cents per bushel (minus commission). Your profit is calculated as the difference between the price you sold the option for and the price you bought back the option for.

As an investor, you might be thinking of other ways to make a profit using options. You could decide to take the risk of making a bigger profit by allowing your option to expire, hoping that December wheat options reach more than $4.00 before the expiration of your options in November. If December wheat options rise above $4.00, your buyer would most likely exercise the call and your options would become unprofitable.

To prevent this type of financial loss as an investor, you would be careful to sell options when you are sure that they won't be exercised or when you are certain that the loss you make on the exercised options position would be less than whatever premium you receive. No matter how sure you are, investing in options as an options seller will always carry with it a certain risk of loss. You can try to mitigate your risk by studying the market and selling your options at the rigjt time (when time value is decreasing). As an investor, waiting for an option to expire or to be exercised can backfire because the option could end up out of the money. Since you can never accurately predict the market, selling options as a hedging strategy will always be a risky investment, unlike buying options.

Chapter Summary

- Stakeholders make a profit from the options market in different ways.
- Businesses and individuals in the agribusiness sector of processing and manufacturing are very interested in trading (buying) agricultural commodities.
- Farmers and feedlot managers use the options market as a way to protect themselves from the fluctuations of the exchange.

- The actions and motivations of individual stakeholders in the options exchange market keeps the market alive, well-regulated and well-managed.
- Options contracts are mainly used by investors to hedge against risks in their already existing investments.
- Options are used as a secondary way of making money by investors because they can be a very profitable form of investing.
- Implied volatility is a great way to estimate option prices in real time. Think of implied volatility as a financial metric for calculating/predicting the likelihood of changes/fluctuations in a given option's price.
- For investors, implied volatility is a great metric to use to predict which options will most likely be profitable and which ones won't.
- Implied volatility will increase when the options market sees a downtrend because options are seeing less trade and less movement between owners.
- The "expected move" of any financial security is how much a stock is expected/predicted to fall or rise from its current market price. The expected move is based on the security's current level of implied volatility.
- Standard deviation is used to calculate expected move because the price of underlying assets is always going either up or down on the market - usually moving up or down in the same direction for consecutive days.
- With high implied volatility, there are wild swings in market prices over the next 12 months (or until its expiration date), with a higher likelihood of making both a loss and a profit.
- A bearish market most often leads to high implied volatility.
- A bullish market most often leads to low implied volatility.

- You can usually find out the implied volatility and historical volatility of your option from your broker or on the option chain section of your broker platform.
- The simplest market changes will cause implied volatility to either increase or decrease. If you want your options to yield higher premiums then pay attention to the implied volatility of your options before investing. Keep a constant watch on market trends, financial and political news and other current or emergency events.
- Implied volatility based entirely on market prices ignores fundamentals in the process.
- Historical volatility measures past market fluctuations. It offers a quantitative way to understand how underlying securities perform on the market by analysing price change fluctuations over a period of time.
- HV is a less popular metric than implied volatility because it requires more effort and financial and mathematical know-how.
- Although an underlying asset can have just one volatility, this does not translate to every option contract on the same underlying asset.
- As a trader, it is in your best interest to use both implied and historical volatility. Used together, they will both significantly reduce your chances of a bad trade.
- Trading at just the perfect time is one unpredictable part of the financial market.
- The IV rank allows you to rank/measure whether the implied volatility of an underlying asset is high or low relative to, not just its level in the past, but also relative to other options.
- Most investors use both IV and IV rank to get a fuller picture of a stock's volatility.
- Concurrently, using the IV rank can sometimes oversimplify your market choices.

- If an earnings (or any other business) announcement is upcoming, you might want to wait until the market stabilizes before making an investment.
- IV and IV rank will work fine most of the time, but not all of the time. It is in your best interest to use IV and IV rank as part of a comprehensive strategy, and one of many deciding factors for making market plays.
- The IV percentile is one of the most common metrics used for measuring and ranking stock prices.
- Speculative trading in the options and futures commodity market is very popular because it offers speculators a high level of leverage.
- Speculative traders and the options commodity market have a mutually beneficial relationship.

In the next chapter you will learn how commodity options differ from stock options.

Chapter 4

How Does Commodity Options Differ From Stock Options?

At this point in the book you might be wondering what the difference between a commodity option and a stock option is. After all, they both deal in the investment and the profitability of the financial market. Nonetheless, commodity options are quite different from stock options. This chapter will highlight the key differences between the two, to give you a sense of why options might be the better choice to meet your financial needs.

The first difference you should know is that stocks deal with investing in a piece of a company. It is a direct investment into the shares of a company for the sole purpose of making a profit. When you purchase a stock you essentially own a piece of the company. Depending on how many shares you purchase you can then be said to own a particular amount of the company based on what each share merits. For example purchasing 100 shares may mean that you now own 0.00001% of the company. Since you are now a part owner of the company you also are entitled to earnings, profits, losses and assets. There are two types of stocks: common stocks and preferred stocks.

Common Stocks

When you own common stocks you are entitled to a proportionate share of the company's profits or losses. As a stockholder you can also decide on policies and any other future decisions related to the company. For example, common stockholders determine and elect the Board of Directors of their company. They can also decide to force a Board of director out of the company. As part owner of common stocks, you have your say in all business decisions that the company makes. Likewise, the Board of Directors decides whether to hold on to, or release, some or all of the company's profits back to stockholders, in the form of dividends.

Preferred Stocks

When you purchase preferred stocks, your dividends are paid out in a more specific manner. That is you have a predetermined time when your dividends are paid out to you. It may be, for example, that dividends of preferred stocks are paid out to stockholders of the company every two years. Preferred stockholders always come first before common stockholders. Preferred stock is always paid out before common stock, for example. Similarly, if a company goes bankrupt, as the title betrays, preferred stockholders are given preferred treatment over common stockholders. That means that preferred stockholders, in this situation, are much more likely to gain back their investment profits over common stockholders.

Whether you have preferred or common stocks (or both) as a stock owner, you have voting rights. It's also very important to note that stocks have no expiration date. You own them for as long as the company exists. Indeed, stocks can be passed down as an inheritance. In that way, stocks have a lot more permanence, as opposed to commodity options, where options usually trade ownership within months. Since stocks are investments into companies, they are less perishable than commodity options. Commodities expire quickly and must be sold, bought and used within a short period of time. Take for example, crude oil, oats, beans, and so on. An option holder of these commodities cannot hold them for years because they will have lost their purpose by then. Since the value of these commodities is in the purpose they serve, they must be traded while they still hold a purpose. In essence, stock options can be said to be a more long-term or, at the very least, longitudinal investment. That is, a stockholder would very likely prefer to hold their stock for years before attempting to sell. While stock prices can and do shoot up within the space of months, most stockholders would not be willing to sell even when this occurs because regaining that stock could prove to be expensive in the future. Based on this key model difference between the two, commodity options, therefore, offer less risk and a greater chance of profit when investors use it to hedge.

From this we see that stock options are an asset while commodity options can become an expense if they expire out-of-the-money. Commodity options cannot be considered an asset because you lose the obligation to buy once it has expired. The only way a commodity option becomes an asset is if you choose to purchase the physical commodity, wherein the asset is physically delivered to you.

A stock option is an obligation and a right to buy. A commodity option, on the other hand, is a right to buy without the obligation, as discussed in **Chapter One**. You have to purchase a stock option to get a right to buy, but you don't have to do the same with a commodity option if you don't want to. Without purchasing a stock option you cannot make a profit from it, but you can still make a profit without purchasing a commodity option (minus paying for the premium). Since you purchase both the obligation and the right to buy stock options, you do get more ownership over your stock. For those who seek more ownership, stock options are a better choice. For example, imagine that you have bought a position in 1,000 bushels of oats. The oats are not ready yet because it is not harvest season. You hope that the farmer would be able to harvest good quality oils. Since you only have the right to buy, but not the obligation, you cannot tell the farmer how to raise his crops. Perhaps if he uses hydroponics he can get better quality oats however, you cannot enforce this decision, neither do you have a say in it. You have no control over whether or not you make a profit. When you own stocks in a company, on the other hand, you can choose to vote on whether or not you like the methods or decisions of a particular CEO, for example. You have more control over the future of the company, as well as the methods in which the company uses to make profit. Even better, as a shareholder, you receive dividends on your stock. With commodity options your profits are a singular occurrence. With stock options, you gain regular profits (or losses) because you own a share of the company.

Nonetheless, there are outside forces that influence both stock options and commodity options. In the case of stock options, these are often company fundamentals, for example, company earning outlooks. If the company is predicted to make a lot of profits, then stock prices go up. If a company's products and services are very popular and successful then stock prices will also go up. The positive engagement that stakeholders have with the company, the more stock prices go up. The company's public relations are very positive, then stock prices will equally go up. For instance, news of a merger with another powerful company will obviously drive stock prices up as shareholders seek to buy shares in a company that they predict will be very successful in the future. News of a merger with a less successful or efficient company will, conversely, drive share prices down as shareholders try to get rid of this stock which they predict will lose much of its value. If a company launches a very successful product, then stock prices will naturally go up as shareholders seek to partake in some of the company's success. While shareholders can vote on matters related to the company, there are so many other outside forces (usually tied to the company itself) that can still determine share prices. This is why companies are very particular about the business decisions that they make.

Commodity options cannot work like this because you purchase your position not from big companies on international stock markets, but usually from smaller individuals and much smaller companies. A farmer's wheat will not suddenly go up in price because he merged with another farm, nor will the farmer's professional/business reputation affect the price of his wheat crops. What usually affects the price of commodity options are industry-wide, international outside events, as already discussed previously. That is, a bad wheat harvest in a country that produces a significant amount of the world's wheat would cause wheat commodity option prices to rise for the next year. Commodity option prices are based on the price of underlying assets, time to expiration and other inside market factors. You can argue that commodity options trading is an ecosystem of itself, not too heavily influenced by outside market forces, as stock options are. However if you are purchasing commodities where a trader is an international company, then their fundamentals could affect option prices. A good example is the oil industry. Key traders are specific nations and global companies. Therefore, decisions made by these companies will affect the prices of oil options directly.

Another unfortunate difference between commodity options trading and stock trading is that you cannot trade your commodity option stocks after it expires. You have a limited time to buy, sell or offset your position. Actually, you have a limited time to make serious financial decisions. This may not be in your best interest especially if you prefer to take your time to make financial and investment decisions. You feel rushed to make a decision and, unfortunately, you cannot do anything to rectify it once your position expires. Naturally, you have more time to make decisions with stocks because you own them for a much longer period of time. Stocks and more permanent by design. You can sell your stock to a buyer at any point in time and you can buy stocks from a buyer at any point in time. There is more decision making and trading power with stocks. Yet, this decision-making power comes with its own disadvantages too.

With greater power comes greater responsibility. With more responsibility comes more risk. When you purchase stock options, you could lose your entire principal investment. Market dips could cause you to lose it all, even in a space of a day, as we saw during the great recession of the 1930s. Course this is one of the best advantages of investing in options. No matter the market dip, you are guaranteed to save your money because you already have the right to buy at a particular strike price. You do risk the entire amount of premium that you pay but this is a small sacrifice for the freedom you gain from not purchasing the option outright from the outset. . This is, of course, if you are an option holder, meaning that you have purchased an option position. In **Chapter Three's** real life examples, you see that options writers (i.e. sellers) face much more risk in the market. While it is a great way to lock in the price of your product when you believe that prices are about to fall, iit is also a great strategy for losing money if your predictions are wrong and prices suddenly skyrocket. This is especially important because the market includes no cap on how high commodity options can go. This means you take a risk losing as an options seller everytime you sell your stocks.

Based on the differences I described above you can see that purchasing stock is like betting with the company. Both you, and the company, are expecting, hoping and doing the best that you can to see profits go up and to reduce your likelihood of loss. Commodity options are in complete contrast to this. Both the seller and the buyer are essentially betting against each other. Think about it. If you, as a buyer, make a profit on your commodity options, that means that the seller either breaks even or makes less money than they would have made had they not locked in the price - since you bought the stock at a cheaper strike price. On the other hand, if you, as a seller, make a profit, it is because the buyer either breaks even or makes less money than they would have since they bought your options for a much larger amount than the strike price at the time of expiration. You are both speculating that stock option prices would either appreciate or depreciate so that you can make a profit at the expense of the other person, despite not taking full responsibility of stock ownership.

Some people in the financial world argue that stock options are a more traditional form of investment. However that is not necessarily true. As you see from the history of commodity options, they have been used as a form of investment for centuries. Undeniably, stock options are the more popular form of investment. Nonetheless, investing in commodity options is becoming more popular, as people see it as an alternative form of investing. It offers less responsibility and less rewards but, at the same time, it is a great way to receive one-off profits by investing a smaller amount of money.

You would be right to say both stock options and commodity options are important portfolio tools for any investor, no matter where you are in your investment journey. The only difference is the purpose of both investment options. Whereas stocks are great for long-term, solid and more risky investments, options are great for short-term, flexible and less risky investments. Hence, although you can invest in stock options as a beginner investor, I would recommend you begin with commodity options to give you a sense of what investing in the financial market is like. The flexibility and short-term benefits of commodity options offers you a safer environment to get your very first experience as a baby investor.

Chapter Summary

- Commodity options and stock options are quite different even though they both deal in the investment and the profitability of the financial market.
- Stocks are a direct investment into the shares of a company for the sole purpose of making a profit.
- When you purchase a stock you essentially own a piece of the company.
- There are two types of stocks: common stocks and preferred stocks. Whether you have preferred or common stocks (or both), as a stock owner, you have voting rights.
- Unlike commodity options, stock options have no expiration date.
- A stock option is an obligation and a right to buy. A commodity option, on the other hand, is a right to buy without the obligation.
- Without purchasing a stock option you cannot make a profit from it, but you can still make a profit without purchasing a commodity option (minus paying for the premium).
- Without purchasing a stock option you cannot make a profit from it, but you can still make a profit without purchasing a commodity option (minus paying for the premium).
- There is more decision making and trading power with stocks.
- Undeniably, stock options are the more popular form of investment.
- Investing in commodity options is becoming more popular, as people see it as an alternative form of investing. It offers less responsibility and less rewards but, at the same time, it is a great way to receive one-off profits by investing a smaller amount of money.

- Whereas stocks are great for long-term, solid and more risky investments, options are great for short-term, flexible and less risky investments.
- The flexibility and short-term benefits of commodity options offers you a safer environment to get your very first experience as a baby investor.

In the next chapter you will learn how commodity options trading works.

Chapter 5

How Does Commodity Option Trading Work?

Now that you know how commodity options markets work the next step this book will teach you is understanding how commodity options trading actually works. What that means is how do you actually trade commodity options on the market? How do investors like you keep the market afloat through commodity trading?

Taking A Short Position In Options

Also known as shorting a stock or short selling, taking a short stock position is the process of selling a stock option that you don't actually hold in your portfolio. You borrow the stock, then sell it for profit. You then hold on to the profit you make, waiting for prices to go down, before then buying back the stock and returning it to the owner who you borrowed it from. The difference from your profits and buying back the stock is then yours to keep.

Short selling is a bearish investment tactic that typically involves borrowing from your broker who lends you options from their own inventory. If this is not possible, they will lend you options from another broker's inventory, or from other clients who are willing to lend their stock options because they have margin accounts.

To hold a short position you must have an account with a brokerage or a broker. Options' short selling margin requirement works just like marginal requirements of future exchanges (as I discussed earlier in the book). Essentially, your broker will ask you to meet their initial and maintenance margin requirements. So, if your broker requires a 40% margin requirement on shorted stocks, you will need $2,000 in your account to be able to open a $5,000 short position. You will also be obligated to make dividend payments on your shorted stock to the lender. This is how the lender makes money from renting out their stocks. In basic terms, holding a short position works similarly to subletting an apartment. However, in the case of short selling, you predict you will benefit from future options depreciation, enabling you to make a profit in the process.

Yes, short selling is a bearish investment move, but it is a very risky one because investment markets do tend to swing towards appreciation. In this case you will then have to close your position, making a loss from your gamble. If you want to short sell, you really need to understand the market to be able to pinpoint beneficial trends in the market that you use for your profit, such as disappointing earnings reports or adverse news events. It is always best, in that case, to use short selling for speculation and hedging.

Imagine you want to hedge using a short position. You own your own stock positions, but do not want to sell because you believe they will appreciate in price in the next six months. Concurrently, you have seen an adverse news story that allows you to predict depreciating prices in the next few weeks. Rightfully so you don't want to sell your stock options. They may depreciate in value soon but they will still appreciate in the next 6 months. Your best strategy is to hold and then hedge you and then hedge using a short position so that you can make a problem so that you can make a profit in the short term.

On the other hand, you may hear that peanut options are about to depreciate in price because of overproduction. It is currently being sold at $1.50 a bushel, so you short 1,000 bushels for $1,500. As you predicted, peanut prices do fall to $1.00 per bushel. You then buy back 1,000 bushels at $1,000, replacing the one you borrowed. Excluding dividends and interests, you have made a $500 profit in just a few weeks.

Here is where speculating becomes risky. If your predictions are wrong and peanut option prices go up to $2.00 per bushel, you have made a $500 loss.

Taking A Long Position In Options

When you take a long position in an options contract, you take a leap of faith that the options will increase substantially in value over the long term. You are a bearish investor, essentially believing your options will give you very good returns after a long time. This is usually based on your own research, or your broker's research on the particular commodity at that particular time. As already discussed in **Chapter Two**, a long position can either be a long call option or a long put option. Another reason people purchase long call options or long put options is because they want to sell it for a higher price in the future. Let's take a look at an example.

Your broker advises that crude oil will increase to $140 per barrel in about 6 months. Crude oil is selling today for $100 a barrel, so you purchase a long call option contract for 100 barrels, set to expire in six months, at a strike price of $100 per barrel, and a premium fee of $4 per barrel for the option itself. In five months, oil has gone up to $160 per barrel. You decide to exercise your option and buy 100 barrels at $100 each. Then, you sell them for $160 each, making you a profit of $5,600 once you pay off your premium fee.

The same process occurs with long put options. If you think a commodity's option will drop sooner or later, you can purchase a long put option contract that will grant you the right to sell shares of that option in the future at the current price at the time of purchase from the buyer. Let us see another example. Your broker advises that corn will decrease to $3.25 per bushel in about 4 months. Corn is selling today for $4.00 a bushel, so you purchase a long pull option contract for 50 bushels, set to expire in four months, at a strike price of $0.10 per bushel, and a premium fee of $2 per bushel. In three months, corn has gone down to $3.00 per bushel. You decide to exercise your option and buy 50 bushels at $3.00 each. Then, once the price goes up once more, you sell them for $4.25 each, making you a profit of $77.50 once you pay off your premium fee.

Exiting An Option

There are three ways to exit an options contract once it has been traded. They are:

1. Exercising the option.
2. Offsetting the option.
3. Allowing the option to expire.

Exercising The Option

If you choose to enforce your right to buy or sell your underlying security at its fixed price, you are said to be exercising your option. Exercising your option can be a complex process, but one that you will need to know for when you decide to exercise your option. While the process relies mostly on other stakeholders in the commodities market to play their part, it is still important for you to know how the system works, so you can monitor your investment every step of the way.

As has been previously mentioned, you can make a profit on your options positions without exercising them. In fact, as a beginner trader, you should be aware that most commodities investors make a profit from closing their positions and then buying and selling options. Nonetheless, exercising your options can be occasionally profitable too. There are a few reasons why you may want or need to exercise your options, for example, exercising your option if you truly want to own the underlying security. Here's an example:

You purchase options on a particular commodity speculatively because you expect the price to go up in a few months. After a few months the price has, indeed, skyrocketed. Although selling would make a nice short haul profit, you decide you would like to use the commodity, after all, for business purposes. Or, perhaps, you decide, based on the market, that you will make even more profit if you hold for another few months. Rather than speculating, you pivot to a long term position. In both instances, you will need to exercise your option, whereby you buy the options at the favorable strike price and then either keep or hold the underlying asset.

Another reason to exercise your option is if you bought options positions as a complementary investment to bring you returns while you invested in the stock market. If your stocks did not do well, you may seek to exercise your put options to gain a profit.

Before I get into how to exercise your option, be aware that having the right reason and strategy for exercising your option is often what will lead to profitable returns. At the same time, be aware that exercising your options can be much more costly than simply selling them. You will have to pay commissions, whether you are exercising your call options before then selling the underlying security or are buying the underlying security before then exercising your put options. Your costs are likely to be noticeably higher than the costs of simply selling the contracts for a profit. Additionally, exercising your contract dictates that the extrinsic value of your options is lost immediately. This is particularly important to note because if you have an options contract that is in-the-money, you have a position that is profitable once you exercise it. However, you will only receive the intrinsic value when exercised. If you decide to sell it, on the other hand, you will receive the benefits of both the intrinsic and extrinsic value.

Once you purchase an option and have decided you want to exercise it, you have to contact your broker and instruct them to proceed with exercising it. If your broker is online, you can also click on the "Exercise Options" button online or on the app to begin the process.

After your broker receives this instruction, they will submit an exercise notice to a relevant clearing house. In the United States, you can use The Options Clearing Corporation (OCC) or The Board of Trade Clearing Corporation (BTCC). The name of the clearing house will be different, depending on your country and region. The OCC, for instance, is the biggest clearing house in the United States. Nevertheless, they all have the same function: to settle investment contracts.

The BTCC (or whichever clearing house you choose) exercises your option by creating a new futures position at the strike price for a new potential option buyer. Upon receiving the exercise notice, the clearing house will seek a member who has previously written these contracts (i.e. is short on the exercised contract). The goal of the clearing house in this step of the process is to find a member firm as quickly as possible. Once one is chosen, the responsibility then passes on to the member firm.

At this point, the selected member firm now has the responsibility of fulfilling the terms of the contract. If your exercised option is a call option, the firm has to deliver the underlying position. If your exercised option is a put option, the firm has to pay for the underlying security. Once it achieves this, the firm will seek an account holder who is short on the exercised contract and issue them an assignment*. The assignment can be issued to anyone who has written specific contracts. Once issued, an assignment means that the account holder has to legally fulfil the terms of the contracts they previously wrote.

The pathway to exercising your option in your country will be mostly similar. Your first step will always be to contact your broker regardless of where you live. The clearing house then carries out the exercise that night. In fact, the process is a very swift one, despite sounding very complicated. You are likely to see the end product (net profits) in your trading account by the following business day.

Offsetting The Option

The second opportunity available to you is to offset your options. Offsetting is the most popular method that investors use to close out their options position. It works by allowing you to reverse your trade as a way of exiting your options contract. If you want to officially exit your trade you must offset your option. If you want to recover any leftover time value on your contract, you must also offset your option before expiration. This is your only option for recovering time value. To reverse the trade all you need to do is sell an option that you originally bought or buy back an option that you originally sold. You have until the last trading day to do so. Your last trading day is the first business day before your options expiration date.

To reverse a call that you bought, you must "sell to close" the exact same call using the same expiration and strike price. Without following these parameters, you cannot close your option. On the other hand if you own a put option, You must "sell to close" the exact same put. Conversely, if you sold a put option, you must "buy to close" using the exact same expiration and strike price. Pay attention to the parameters of setting your up offsetting your option. The expiration and strike price need to be the same otherwise it is not considered closed, even if you have reduced your risk.

Offsetting is the most popular method for closing out an option position because it is the easiest and costs no additional fees.

Offsetting also precludes the risks of having an options position being assigned to you if you already sold an option and would like to avoid any possibilities of having said option exercised against.

Nonetheless you are still bound by fluctuations in the markets at the time you decide to either buy back or sell back. It is possible that there will be no active market for your options at the time you decide to offset. Hence, it is best to watch the market closely around the time you want to offset to ensure that there is actually a market for your commodity at the set strike price. If your option becomes out of the money or is nearing its expiration date, you will also struggle to find a market willing to purchase it., so it is best to offset your option well beforehand.

After offsetting your option a commission will be deducted by your broker, after which you can calculate your net profit or loss. To calculate your net profit or loss, deduct the premium you paid to purchase your option (or the premium you paid to receive to sell your option) from the premium you receive (or the premium you pay) once you offset your options.

Most options holders like to offset their options if it is still in the money and has time value. That is because exercising your option will only give you a yield on its intrinsic value, so you lose out on any remaining time value unless you offset your options. Likewise, paying an extra commission to your broker is another disadvantage that puts off people from exercising their option.

Allowing The Option To Expire

If you allow your options contract to expire you will no longer be able to trade that derivative. Upon an options' expiration (also known as OpEx), options that are out-of-the-money will become worthless. That means no further action is required by you and the contract will simply be removed from your account. Options that are in-the-money will expire to cash if you chose to have your contract cash-settled. Otherwise, expired in-the-money options expire into either long or short shares of stock.

At the same time, an option expiring in-the-money does not mean that you automatically make a profit. It simply means that your option is assigned and the obligations described in the contract are fulfilled. This includes stock obligations, so that the amount of stock specified in your contract will be assigned by either being bought or sold. That means that, if you agreed to buy 300 bushels of wheat, you must pay for it when your option expires. If you agreed to sell 300 bushels of wheat, you must sell it and have it delivered.

Standard OpEx occurs on the third Friday of every month. So, the last day of trade for standard monthly options is the third Friday of every month. This usually falls on the 15th and 21st day of each month. If the last day of trade falls on a market holiday, then the final day of trade for standard monthly options will be on Thursday of the same week.

Non-standard OpEx occurs on any date that is not on the third Friday of the month. These could be options with weekly or quarterly expiration cycles. For weekly OpEx, expiration happens every Friday, except during quarterly expiration weeks. For monthly OpEx, expiration occurs on the last trading day of March, June, September, and December.

As an options investor, you can choose the expiration cycle that you want. Short-term expiration cycles can last as long as 0 days (i.e. expiring on the same day) while the longest expiration cycles can last approximately two years. Longer-term OpExs are usually standard monthlies. Why? Weekly OpEx are not listed until a few weeks before their expiration dates. Trading and expiration dates are very important to note because options lose value the nearer they reach their expiration date. Likewise, if your options reach exploration and you do not have the capital needed to either buy or sell the assigned number of stocks, then it will lead to a margin call. Alternatively, your options position will be forcefully liquified.

It is also important to note that American options work differently from European options. I have only explained what happens when American option contracts expire. In fact I would advise that you research how options work in your country before you begin investing. Different countries have different rules on how options work, so don't assume that the information in this book applies to your country. You can end up making the wrong investment decisions if you do.

For example, American options can be exercised at any time, while European options can only be exercised at expiration. Upon expiration, in-the-money American options settle to stock while in-the-money European options settle to cash. American options will also offer you underlying shares while European ones don't. Remember that the expiration date of your options contract simply represents the last day of your contract's validity.

Finally, don't rule out closing your position before the expiration date. This is the safest way to make a profit from your contract. Simply close your contract when prices are just right (i.e. when a trade works in your favor) and then have your options cash-settled.

Chapter Summary

- Also known as shorting a stock or short selling, taking a short stock position is the process of selling a stock option that you don't actually hold in your portfolio.
- Short selling is a bearish investment tactic that typically involves borrowing from your broker who lends you options from their own inventory.
- To hold a short position you must have an account with a brokerage or a broker.
- Short selling is a very risky move because investment markets do tend to swing towards appreciation.

- When you take a long position in an options contract, you strongly believe that the options will increase substantially in value over the long term.
- Another reason people purchase long call options or long put options is because they want to sell it for a higher price in the future.
- There are three ways to exit an options contract once it has been traded. They are: exercising the option, offsetting the option and allowing the option to expire.
- If you choose to enforce your right to buy or sell your underlying security at its fixed price, you are said to be exercising your option.
- Another reason to exercise your option is if you bought options positions as a complementary investment to bring you returns while you invested in the stock market.
- If your stocks did not do well, you may seek to exercise your put options to gain a profit.
- Having the right reason and strategy for exercising your option is often what will lead to profitable returns
- Exercising your options can be much more costly than simply selling them.
- When exercising your options, Your first step will always be to contact your broker regardless of where you live.
- Offsetting is the most popular method that investors use to close out their options position. It works by allowing you to reverse your trade as a way of exiting your options contract.
- If you want to recover any leftover time value on your contract, you must offset your option before expiration by selling an option that you originally bought or buying back an option that you originally sold.
- If you allow your options contract to expire, you will no longer be able to trade that derivative.
- Upon an options' expiration, options that are out-of-the-money become worthless.

- Options that are in-the-money will expire to cash if you chose to have your contract cash-settled.
- An option expiring in-the-money does not mean that you automatically make a profit.
- An option expiring in-the-money means that your option is assigned and the obligations described in the contract are fulfilled.
- As an options investor, you can choose the expiration cycle that you want.

In the next chapter you will learn how to choose which commodity options to trade.

Chapter 6

What Are Some Commodity Option Strategies?

As a beginner options investor, it can be tempting to hastily begin trading options once you have the basics (covered in previous chapters). However, you should know that there are options strategies you can use to trade successfully with less effort, limited risk and maximized returns. This may seem overwhelming at first, but don't fret! These strategies are simple, yet empowering, allowing you to make a decent profit, hedge your existing positions and bet on market movement.

Here are some commodity options strategies you can use to trade on the market.

1. Covered

In order to make money with a covered call strategy, you must first know what a covered call is. A covered call really is just a financial transaction for an investor who owns options. Ergo, once you own commodity options stock, you have to own the same amount that is equivalent to its underlying security to make a covered call. The options you hold also have to be long positions. Once you hold a long position of an underlying futures contract, you can then sell call options on this asset, with the hope that you make a profit.

A covered call is a sort of gamble. You are hoping to generate an income stream from the premium the buyer pays whilst also hoping the buyer does not choose to exercise their options. If your stock's price does appreciate over the option's strike price, and your buyer chooses to exercise the option, you will have to pay your buyer the stock gains you made and give them, for each contract written, 100 shares at the strike price. Nonetheless, as you have seen in earlier chapters, the expected move probability of options with low implied volatility is very low. Consequently, your risk of the buyer exercising their options is very low.

Likewise, a covered call strategy is not right for you if you prefer bearish or bullish investments, both of which rely on massive market swings. If you are a bullish investor, you will want to hold on to the stock until it appreciates, at which point you make your profit. You wouldn't like the potential of giving some of your profits away to another buyer. If you were a bearish investor, you would sell the stock to make as much of your investment back. The profit you make from a covered call will not make up for your loss if your options depreciate in value even more.

For a covered call to work, you have to be holding a long position with the expectation that your options will not appreciate in the near future. In essence, implied volatility is very low, so your underlying futures price is predicted to stay roughly the same until the short-term. For this reason, covered calls are known as a neutral strategy that allows you to have your cake and eat it: to hold on to your underlying futures contract until it can potentially appreciate while making a profit off its premiums.

I like to think of covered calls as making a short-term hedge on a long stock position. It is similar to purchasing a home on a mortgage, then renting it out for the sole purpose of making short-term profits on a long-term investment.

You must pay attention to how profits and loss work on a covered call as this will affect how much return you see on your investment. For a covered call, the maximum profit is the same as the premium you received when you sold the options. In addition, the profit also includes the difference between the current price and the strike price, if the stock appreciates. The maximum loss is the purchase price of your underlying asset minus the premium received for your call option. It is calculated this way because your underlying asset could drop to zero meaning that the only profit you make is the premium which your buyer paid for the options.

Covered calls are perfect for all investors, regardless of income level. Since you are using it to hedge in the price of your commodity, you can even place a covered call while purchasing your options. This is known as a buy-write transaction, wherein you simultaneously buy a commodity option long position while simultaneously selling call options against that position. If you don't like this option, you have the option of a basic covered call, as examined above. Lastly, you have the option of making a naked call.

2. Naked (Uncovered) Call

A naked call (also known as an unhedged or uncovered call) involves you selling call options in the commodity market without you owning the underlying security. With a naked call, the only profit you receive is the premium. While naked calls are a great way to generate income without investing in owning your own underlying futures contract, it is a high risk endeavour, unlike basic covered calls or buy-write transactions. Not only is your profit potential very low, it rests on the option expiring worthless. Even worse, there is no maximum loss if you choose a naked call. This is because you just can't tell how high the strike price of the underlying asset will rise. In fact, you can bet that the seller of the options will rush to buy them back (exercising their right to purchase their security) if the price of the underlying asset starts to inch too close or above its strike price. That means that you are not even guaranteed to make a profit off your premiums since you will be forced to sell your options back to the seller at a much lower price than the market price.

I would advise you to only use naked call options as an investment strategy only after you have gained a bit more experience investing in the options trading market. At the same time, an uncovered call should only be used if you are certain that the price of the underlying security will fall or stay the same. Needless to say, never use a naked call on stock options with a high implied volatility because it could suddenly swing into profitability, causing the writer (seller) to exercise it and leaving you with no profits.

3. Bull Call Spread

A bull call spread is for bullish investors, as you would guess from the name. It is a strategy for investors who are banking on making a profit from a stock's limited price increase.

For a bull call spread strategy to work, you must first study the market to decide on an asset that you believe will see a small appreciation over a particular period of time (be it days, weeks, or months).Then, you buy a call option at a strike price that is slightly above current market strike price, ensuring to pay the premium. You then sell a call option with the same expiration date and underlying asset as the call option you just bought, collecting the premium in the process. In essence, you profit from the underlying asset's limited appreciation.

How does this work? You essentially use both call options to form a range from the lower strike price to the upper strike price. You expect a moderate appreciation while counting on the bullish call spread to help limit the losses you incur from owning stock. While limiting loss, a bull call spread also caps your gains. This is a much better strategy than an outright naked call option because you are given the opportunity to make even a little bit of profit. In fact, potential profits are capped, so you have a limited range where you can make a profit.

Bullish investors like to use bull call spreads during times of high volatility. Profits might be limited due to lower and upper strike price, but you still have the opportunity to make some profit despite high volatility.

At OpEx, if the stock price has depreciated below the strike price of the first purchased call option, you will not have to exercise the out-of-the-money option as it will be closed, expiring worthlessly. You will, therefore, lose the premium you paid for it. If you choose to exercise the option, on the other hand, you will have to pay more for what is essentially a security that is worth less in the current market than what you are paying for it.

At OpEx, if the stock price has appreciated above the strike price of the second purchased call option, I.e. in-the-money, you will exercise your first option, buying the stock for less than its current market price. The second call option will still be active at this point, so it would be either assigned or exercised. You can then sell the first options contract to purchase the second options contract. This is why your profit from purchasing the first call option never rises past the strike price of the second.

4. Bear Put Strategy

Also known as a debit put spread or long put spread, a bear put spread strategy is very similar to a bull call spread strategy. From the differences and similarities between their names, you can already decipher how similar and different these two strategies are. Simply put, one strategy favours bearish investors, while the other strategy favours bullish investors. In a bear put strategy, you are focused on making a profit from depreciating stock option prices. Whereas a bull put strategy focuses on making a profit from appreciating put stock option prices.

A bearish investor uses a bear put strategy to purchase put options, only to then sell, at a lower price, the same number of puts on the same underlying asset, and with the same exact expiration date. Your profit will, therefore, be the difference between both put strike prices (minus their net costs, of course). This means that you only make a profit if the price of the underlying asset depreciates.

Bear put spread strategies are certainly less risky than holding a short position, however, like a bull call spread, your profit is limited to the difference in your strike price.

Let's take an example: You purchase a put option contract of 100 bushels of cassava at $2.75 ($275) for a strike price of $15. You then sell 100 bushels of cassava at $0.75 ($75) foer a strike price of $10. In this bull put spread, you will pay $200 to set it up. If the OpEx of cassava closes below $10, your profit is: ($15 - $10 (the difference between both strike prices)) x 100 bushels - $200 (the net price of both put options. In this case, you make $300 profit.

5. Married Put Strategy

Also known as a protective put, in a married put option strategy, you hold both stock options and a put contract for said stock options. You figuratively "marry" the two to protect your risk of holding on to said stock.

A married put strategy is a bullish hedge. That means that it is typically used to protect an investor who wants to benefit from appreciating asset prices. This strategy acts as a type of insurance to protect you from price changes. Let's take an example of how it works in practice:

You want to buy barrels of oil at $100 a barrel. You purchase 10 barrels then purchase the put option at $90 with a $5 premium. Oil prices then rise to $160 per barrel, which means you can sell the options back for a profit, although you won't get back your $5 premium. You don't need to exercise the put option in this case, since you will gain nothing from it, so you let it expire, losing the $5 premium. On the other hand, if oil prices then dip to $84, you may decide to exercise your option before you lose any money.

This means you lose your $5 premium as well as $6 per barrel. While you make a loss, since you purchased a put option, you can theoretically pull out before you lose any more money.

These are just a few commodity option strategies available to you. There are more strategies that you will learn as you gain more experience. The trick is not to rush anything. Take each strategy one at a time, practising each very well, so that you know all of the in and outs of said strategy, before moving on to practising the next.

Options trading is a marathon, not a sprint. You will get to the finish line and win your medal if you go slow and steady. If you rush the race, you may hurt yourself and never get to reach the finish line.

Slow and steady wins the race!

Chapter Summary

- There are options strategies you can use to trade successfully with less effort, limited risk and maximized returns.
- Once you own commodity options stock, you have to own the same amount that is equivalent to its underlying security to make a covered call. The options you hold also have to be long positions.
- A covered call is a gamble. that you generate an income stream from the premium the buyer pays whilst also hoping the buyer does not choose to exercise their options.
- A covered call does not rely on bullish or bearish investments, i.e. it does not rely on massive market swings. They should be considered a neutral strategy: a short-term hedge on a long stock position.

- An uncovered (naked) call involves you selling call options in the commodity market without you owning the underlying security.
- Naked calls are a great way to generate income without investing in owning your own underlying futures contract. They are a high risk endeavour since there is no cap on how much you can lose.
- Use naked call options as an investment strategy only after you have gained a bit more experience investing in the options trading market and only if you are certain that the price of the underlying security will fall or stay the same.
- A bull call spread is for bullish investors. It is a strategy for investors who are banking on making a profit from a stock's limited price increase.
- In a bear put strategy, you are focused on making a profit from depreciating stock option prices as a bearish investor.
- Bear put spread strategies are less risky than holding a short position, but your profit is limited to the difference in your strike price.
- In a married put option strategy, you hold both stock options and a put contract for said stock options.

Final Words

In today's unstable financial market, it is becoming harder and harder to know what to invest in and what to forgo. With so much uncertainty, one thing is clear: the options market is still a great venture for motivated financiers like yourself to make profits!

You read this book because you want to invest in, and play, the options market. The first thing you must do is congratulate yourself for taking this first step to learn! In a perfect world, we'd all be taught how to make money and improve our lives through financial investment. But, you haven't let that stop you! Your motivation has driven you to read this book to learn the differences between futures and options and which better suit your financial and investment needs; the differences between commodity options and stock options; good options strategies to make financially savvy decisions; how to make options trading profitable; how to get started trading options and how to find a reputable commodity broker.

The hard part is over now. You have studied hard, improved your knowledge and learnt the basic skills you need to start your journey into becoming a financial wizard in the options market. Whether as a strategy to make side income or full-time income, this book has given you the tools you need to begin harvesting dollars with options on seasonal agricultural commodities. You don't need to start scrambling through webpage after webpage or book after book to find answers on how to harvest dollars from the comfort of your home! With the information I have brought you in this book, whether it be speculating, hedging or studying volatility, you can make the most profit by predicting the market and then making savvy financial decisions worthy of any Wall Street banker!

Lastly, I want to remind you to start slow. Test the waters with small investments that you can afford to make a loss on. Indeed, you can also make what I like to refer to as "phantom investments," where you make investments without actually playing the market. This gives you the safety of knowing you won't make a loss, but also the time to develop the experience and confidence you need to finally take on the market. If in doubt, speak to your broker and get some advice. Remember that nobody can ever fully predict the market with complete certainty, so don't beat yourself up during those moments when you make a loss. They are simply learning experiences for you to get better at options trading! At the same time, enjoy the profits and invest them back when opportunity comes a-knocking!

That being said, I wish you the best of luck as you begin your new financial journey. May you always buy low (or rent low) and sell high!

Glossary

This glossary is created to help you navigate the exciting new world of options trading. Educating yourself about options trading can be a daunting task. It is an entirely new field and industry and, if you're not familiar with it, the words alone can cause you significant setbacks.

Furthermore, it can require a lot of energy to constantly switch tabs or apps, to look up words. When you do, in fact, look up words, many times you are led to websites or financial dictionaries that cater solely to the already financially literate. Their word definitions can be just as complex and obscure as the words that you searched for in the first place, making the definitions useless and the whole process obsolete.

I want to make this process of learning about options trading efficient, useful and much more beginner-friendly for you. That is why I created a glossary of common terms used in commodity options trading. I have simplified word definitions to simple English, so that you'll be able to understand what the words mean in their financial context.

In many cases the words in this glossary have been used in this book. In other cases, while the words have not been used in a book, they have been included because they are common words and terms used in the industry. You will eventually run into these words as you begin your journey as an investor. Hence, this glossary works as a handsy glossary to empower you with the meaning of key terms. As you come into contact with new words on your investment journey, you can come back to this glossary as many times as you need to remind you of the meanings of common financial words in the options trading market.

As an added bonus, if you already know what the words mean before you encounter them, you can take it in stride once you begin an investment portfolio.

At-the-money: At-the-money (ATM) options can be defined as options with strike prices that are of the same value as the market price of the options' current underlying stock. This is the same for call options and put options.

Assignment: If you are the writer of a contract, an assignment legally requires that you fulfil your obligations as determined by the terms of the contract. For instance, the contract could state that you have to purchase the underlying security in the case where you have written calls. Conversely, the contract could state that you have to sell the underlying security in the case where you have written puts. Your brokerage firm will issue an assignment notice in the circumstances that you have a contract to fulfil.

Bearish Market: This refers to market prices depreciating over time (or traders investing on the prediction that they will). Examples of bearish markets include: short call options and covered pulls.

Black Swans: A probabilistically rare and unpredictable market crash that causes huge financial damage to the market. Since they are unpredictable, typical metrics of measurement, such as implied volatility, are not able to predict them. A good example of a black swan is the house price crash during the 2008 recession.

Broker: A financial broker is a firm or individual who acts as a third party between a seller and buyer during financial transactions of financial assets (the sale of securities).

Bullish Market: This refers to market prices rising over time (or traders investing on the prediction that they will). Examples of bullish markets include: long call options and covered calls.

Bushel: A unit of measurement used in options and futures trading, measuring 35.2 liters (in US measurements) and 36.4 liters (in UK measurements).

Call Option: A call option is an option that gives you (the option buyer) the right to buy (or going long) the underlying futures of an option.

Clearing House: The clearing house acts as an intermediary between the buyer and the seller of stocks. The clearing house ensures that both parties are protected in the sale of the commodity. This means that both parties are guaranteed to get what is their due, as defined by the contract: the buyer gets their asset/shares (or the profits from that asset/shares) while the seller gets their payment.

Commodity Price Index: Commodity price indexes track the price of (and therefore return on) commodities investments. These investments are usually composed into what is known as a basket of commodities. Indexes are useful for investors who want to add commodities to their investment portfolio without doing the work of researching and adding them as individual commodities. The value of commodity indexes fluctuate depending on their underlying commodity. Different commodity indexes also vary: the commodities they comprise of vary, as well as the way they are weighted. For some commodity indexes, each commodity shares an equal percentage of the index. Other indexes are given a predetermined and fixed weighting scheme where an index may have a value that is a higher percentage for a specific commodity.

Contract Size: The contract size is the quantity of the commodity (or asset) of each contract. The construct size is standardized in the market, meaning that it does not change for each commodity. For instance, one contract size of crude oil equals 1,000 barrels.

Delivery: Delivery is simply the transfer of the commodity you purchased or sold, as defined by your contract. It is very common in derivative contracts, such as options and futures, but can also be used to transfer other forms of assets, such as cash, currency and so on. Delivery of futures contracts can be physically-settled-contracts which result in the physical transfer of the commodity after expiry. However, most futures contracts are cash-settled-contracts that will be directly transferred into cash immediately after expiry.

Derivative: A derivative contract means that the value in the contract is agreed-upon by all parties of the contract and based on an asset with financial value.

Elevator Operator: In agriculture, elevators hold and store most of the commodities bought and sold. Thanks to advancement in technology, some elevators can now hold up to 20 million (435000 Metric Ton) bushels of grain. Elevator operators manage these elevators and ensure that commodities are stored, transported and managed in optimum conditions.

Exercise (Your Options): This is the action taken by the holder of a call option who wants to purchase the underlying futures. Exercising your options comes with a few disadvantages, but can be profitable if done for.the right reasons.

Expiration Date: This is the last day you have to exercise your option. The expiration date is always a month before the commodity's delivery month. That means that September corn options will expire in August. Likewise, March wheat options will expire in February. If you are not sure of the expiration date of your options contract, contact your broker or check your brokerage portal.

Feedlot Managers: Feedlot managers manage the feed yard on large farms. They have a distinct set of knowledge to help them with their responsibilities. This includes: herd nutrition, environmental conditions for herds to thrive m, making trades on the options exchange market and marketing.

Fundamentals: Fundamentals refers to basic quantitative and qualitative information that helps build a company's/market's/security's/currency's financial and/or economic well-being. Fundamentals also contribute to the financial valuation of companies, markets, securities and currencies. They include things like management experience, statistics, finances, managerial decisions and so in. Fundamentals are a standard metric for predicting the future of a company, market, security, currency, and so on.

Futures Contracts: Futures contracts work very similar to options contracts. They are contracts traded on a futures exchange. Buyers of futures contracts will have their commodity delivered at a future time, according to the contract's specificities, including its terms and conditions of delivery.

Going-Long: Going long is a term used in options trading to mean you own either a call or put option. A long position refers to purchasing a long call option or a long put option. A long call or put option reveals an optimism in the buyer or seller that their options will do very well in the long-term.

Hedge: To hedge in the price of a commodity is simply to lock in the price of the commodity. By agreeing on a sell/buy price that does not change significantly, both the buyer and seller protect themselves from wild fluctuations in market prices, thereby cutting their risk. Options contracts are hedge investments because they require a stakeholder to enter a legal obligation to buy or sell a commodity at an agreed-upon price at a later date.

In-the-money: In-the-money (ITM) options can be defined as options with strike prices that are of lesser value as the market price of the options' current underlying stock. This is true for call options. For put options, in-the-money options are determined to have a strike price of greater value as the market price of the options' current underlying stock. An in-the-money option is a profitable one, especially when sold.

Intraday: Simply meaning "within-the-day", intraday is also a way of referring to securities that trade on the markets during regular business hours. For short-term investors and day traders, tracking intraday price movements is a very important method for making profit.

Intrinsic Value: The intrinsic value is the amount you get if you exercise your option immediately, i.e. the option's current value at any time. The intrinsic value is the most basic value of an option.

For in the money options, the intrinsic value of the option is a profit to the owner of the option. For example, a $40 call option on a $50 stock would be $10 in the money. If the buyer decides to exercise the option $10 in the money, she can buy the stock at $40 from the option. Since the option is at $50, she can then sell it on the commodities market for that price, getting a $10 payoff. To calculate the intrinsic value of an in the money option, find the difference of the current price of its underlying asset and the strike price of the option.

The intrinsic value of options that are out of the money or at the money is zero. Why? Buyers don't exercise options that result in a loss. When options are at the money or out of the money, a buyer would allow their option to expire, resulting in no payoff. Therefore, the intrinsic value is zero.

To calculate the intrinsic value of a call option, subtract the strike price from the price of the underlying asset. To calculate the intrinsic value of a put option, subtract the price of the underlying asset from the strike price.

Leverage: Financial leverage involves using borrowed capital to invest. The investor hopes that the high risk involved will result in big profit. At the same time, leverage allows investors to generate a bigger buying power. With leverage, you make a small investment, which ends up controlling a large amount of notional value. In the case your investment makes a loss, this means that you now have to pay back the borrowed capital with no profits made.

Liquidity: Liquidity refers to how easy it is for a financial asset or security to be turned into cash, without the asset/security losing parts (or all) of its market value.

Long Position: A long position simply means you have purchased shares of stocks and fully own them.

Margin: Set by federal law, the margin is the minimum amount of collateral (whether in cash or securities) that a buyer needs to cover any credit risks during a financial exchange. It is also used to cover the broker's credit risks during a financial exchange. Another definition is to think of margins as the money a buyer must deposit to ensure that a contract can be fulfilled at a future date. In the options market, however, buyers do not need to post margins, since their premiums (which must be fully paid when purchasing an options contract) act as a form of margin.

Margin Call: If the value of your margin account falls below your broker's required amount, tlur broker will demand a margin call. Your broker will demand that you deposit additional money or securities into your brokerage account. Since the securities in your margin account are funded by both your own money and borrowed money from your broker, your broker can demand, once your margin account falls below her/his required minimum (known as the maintenance margin), that it is brought back up to the maintenance margin.

Margin calls will often occur when one or more of your securities in your margin account decreases value, plunging your account below the maintenance margin. If you are not able to deposit marginable securities or additional funds into a margin account to bring it up to the maintenance margin, you will be required to sell some of your assets to do so.

Mean-Reversion: This is when market price extremities and volatility revert back to their mean after a while. In many option-pricing models, volatility is the one variable that is mean reverting. You can think of mean-reverting as the ever-constant market cycle, moving regularly from high, low and mean.

Moneyness: Moneyness tells you how at-the-money, in-the-money and out-of-the-money options are.

Notional Value: Also known as the "contract value", the notional value is simply the contract size of the asset multiplied by its current price. As a result, the notional value of a crude oil that is trading at $77 a barrel will be $77,000.

Offset: Offsetting your options contract is a way to exit your contract. It can only be done before your contract expires. To offset your options, you simply sell an option that you originally bought or buy back an option that you originally sold.

Open Interest: This is the number of options or futures contracts of a particular commodity that have not been exercised, expired, offset or delivered against. .

Options: Within the future's industry, options are a type of contract that gives buyers the right to buy or sell a futures contract at a particular price and for a limited time (before the contract's expiration date). Buyers have the right to buy, but are never under any obligation to exercise that right.

Option Premium: This is simply the current market price of any option contract. It is calculated by adding an options' intrinsic value to its time value.

Out-Of-The-Money: Out-of-the-money (OTM) options can be defined as options with strike prices that are of greater value as the market price of the options' current underlying stock. This is true for call options. For put options, options are determined to have a strike price of lesser value as the market price of the options' current underlying stock. A holder of an out-of-the money option has made a loss on her/his contract.

Position: A position is defined as the amount of assets, properties or securities that you (or a business) owns. By purchasing a new asset, property or security, you take a new position. You are said to take a short position if you hold on to your shares for a few weeks before selling it off or allowing it to expire. You are said to take a long position if you hold on to your shares for a few months before selling it off or allowing it to expire. Futures and options contracts, by nature, typically rely on long positions although, sometimes, they rely on short positions too. Either way, trading in derivative contracts is trading in positions.

Put Option: A put option is an option that gives you (the option buyer) the right to sell (go short) the underlying asset of an option at the strike price specified in the contract (at the time of purchase).

Short Position: A short position means that you owe stock because you have not yet fully paid for it. People with a short position hope that the stock prices go down so that they can purchase it at a cheaper price. Typically, if you are in a short position, you borrow the shares from a brokerage firm in a margin account, hoping to make the delivery in the future when stock prices fall.

Serial Option Months: Serial option months are short-term option contracts that trade for approximately thirty days and expire during months when there are no standard option contracts expiring. So, the standard trading months for corn are: May, July, September, and December. Therefore, the serial option trading months for corn are January, February, April, June, August, October and November.

Serial options can only be listed for trading on the nearby futures contract months. This is very different to standard options which can be listed for both deferred and nearby contract months.

Speculatation: Also known as "speculative trading", speculation is an act of trading an asset that carries significant risk of losing value, but also the potential for high profit yields. Speculative investments focus on assets with significant price fluctuations - this is where the high chance of risk and profit come from. Speculation is typically not a good strategy for long-term investments because of its high risk and volatile nature.

Speculative investors trade options and futures "speculating" that their investment will increase in the future. Speculative investors are more focused on short-term profits. To ensure short-term profits, speculative investors use a strategy of examining the technicalities of market prices. This is in contrast to the long-term investment strategy of analysing an asset or security to determine irs likelihood of making a profit. Speculative investors are very active market traders, since they make their profits from short-term price fluctuations as opposed to buying and holding like long term investors do.

Standard Options: These are traditional options contracts that trade in the same months as their underlying futures.

Stop-Loss: Stop-loss is a tool used to limit loss when trading stocks. Also known as a stop order, a stop-loss is an automatic order to exit you out of your position the moment your stock hits your set stop price. This set stop price is determined by you, according to how much you are willing to lose.

Stop-losses are a great tool not only for preventing loss, but for protecting you from making trade calls in the moment that you nay regret later on. In the heat of the moment, it is alwaus tempting to think that volatility will suddenly swing your way and net you a profit. However, stocks should never be traded on hope, but on predictability, stability and quantitative and qualitative data. A stop order keeps the trading process free of "hope" and based entirely on market facts.

Strike Price: Also known as the exercise prices, the strike price of a derivative contract (futures or options contract) is the set price at which the contract can be sold when it is exercised. When you have put options, the strike price is the price that the security can be sold. When you have call options, the strike price is where the option holder can buy the security. The strike price heavily determines the option value of a derivative contract.

Tick Size: In the financial market, the tick size is the minimum price increment that a specific contract can fluctuate. It shows how much up or down the price of a trading instrument can move on the financial exchange. The tick value of a contract is often quoted in dollars and cents and, sometimes, in fractions of a penny.

Time Value: This is the amount you get once an options premium exceeds its intrinsic value. When an options contract does not have an intrinsic value, its premium is therefore its time value.

The time value is any extra amount an investor is willing to pay above the option's current intrinsic value. People are often willing to pay for the time value because they gamble that the option has enough time to either increase or decrease in value before its reaches expiration. As a result, options that are about to expire have no time value because there isn't enough time for them to either increase or decrease in value.

To calculate the time value of an option, find the difference between its premium and its intrinsic value.

Underlying Asset: An underlying asset is simply the financial asset upon which a derivative's price/value is based.

Underlying Futures Contract: Any futures contract that can be sold or bought by exercising an option.

Volatility: Volatility in the market refers to how risky the market currently is. That is, there is less stability and security for people trading on the market because of huge swings on either side.

Conversely, volatility can also lead to high yields and profit if your stocks swing upwards.

Volume: The number of futures/options contracts purchased during a specific time period.

Writer: The seller of an options contract.

Resources

Agiboo. (2022). A History Of Grain Elevators. Agiboo. https://www.agiboo.com/grain-elevators/.

Blythe, B. (2018, June 7). Fun With Futures: Basics Of Futures Contracts, Futures Trading. The Ticker Tape. https://tickertape.tdameritrade.com/trading/trading-futures-introduction-16680.

Blythe, B. (2022, February 2). How Tick Sizes And Values Vary In Index Futures. Ameritrade. https://tickertape.tdameritrade.com/trading/index-futures-tick-sizes-17630.

Bohen, T. (2022). Stop-Loss: What It Is, Examples, & Top Strategies to Use. Stocks To Trade. https://stockstotrade.com/stop-loss/.

Butker, C. (2022, April 25). Expected Move Explained: Options Trading. Project Finance. https://www.projectfinance.com/expected-move/.

CFI. (2022). Speculation. CFI. https://corporatefinanceinstitute.com/resources/knowledge/trading-investing/speculation/.

Chen, J. (2022, January 4). Margin Call. Investopedia. https://www.investopedia.com/terms/m/margincall.asp.

Chen, J. (2022, January 8). Bull Call Spread. Investopedia. https://www.investopedia.com/terms/b/bullcallspread.asp .

Chen, J. (2022, May 24). Implied Volatility vs. Historical Volatility: What's the Difference? Investopedia. https://www.investopedia.com/articles/investing-strategy/071616/implied-vs-historical-volatility-main-differences.asp.

Encyclopaedia Britannica. (2022). Chicago Board Of Trade. Encyclopaedia Britannica. https://www.britannica.com/topic/Chicago-Board-of-Trade.

Ganti, A. (2022, April 22). Implied Volatility (IV). Investopedia. https://www.investopedia.com/terms/i/iv.asp.

Gavin. (2022). Implied Volatility Percentile. Options Trading IQ. https://optionstradingiq.com/implied-volatility-percentile/.

Gavin. (2022). Options Trading 101 - The Ultimate Beginners Guide To Options. Options Trading IQ. https://optionstradingiq.com/how-to-calculate-the-expected-move-of-a-stock/.

Gavin. (2022). What Is IV Rank And How To Use It. 2022 Guide. Options Trading IQ. https://optionstradingiq.com/what-is-iv-rank-and-how-to-use-it/.

Hayes, A. (2021, September 02). Black-Scholes Model. Investopedia. https://www.investopedia.com/terms/b/blackscholes.asp.

Jaffee, D. (2021, April 24). What Happens When Options Expire? Best Stock Strategy. https://beststockstrategy.com/what-happens-when-options-expire/.

Johnson, H. (2022). History Of Commodities Trading. Be Businessed. https://bebusinessed.com/history/history-commodities-trading/.

Investopedia. (2022). Home. Investopedia. https://www.investopedia.com/.

Lake, R. (2021, November 15). This Options Strategy Bakes In Risk Protection. Smart Asset. https://smartasset.com/investing/married-put.

Luthi, B. (2022, February 13). Pros And Cons Of Options Trading. Experian. https://www.experian.com/blogs/ask-experian/pros-cons-options-trading/.

Majaski, C. (2021, May 29). Fundamentals. Investopedia. https://www.investopedia.com/terms/f/fundamentals.asp.

Martin, M. (2022, May 2). Implied Volatility Explained (The ULTIMATE Guide). Project Finance. https://www.projectfinance.com/implied-volatility-beginners/.

Martin, M. (2022, May 3). When Do Options Expire? | Options Expiration Explained. Project Finance. https://www.projectfinance.com/expiration-options/.

Maverick, J.B. (2022, March 7). How Does Implied Volatility Impact Options Pricing? Investopedia. https://www.investopedia.com/ask/answers/062415/how-does-implied-volatility-impact-pricing-options.asp.

Options Trading. (2022). Glossary. Options Trading. https://www.optionstrading.org/glossary/.

Options Trading. (2022). Home. Options Trading. https://optionstrading.org/.

Paludeter, D. (2022, June 2). What Is A Short Position In Stocks? Simply Explained. Finbold. https://finbold.com/guide/short-position/.

Pines, L. (2022, February 6). Want To Trade The Humble Soybean? Here Are 5 Ways To Do It Online. Commodity. https://commodity.com/soft-agricultural/soybean/trading/.

Price, M. (2021, November 3). What Is An At-The Money Option? The Balance. https://www.thebalance.com/what-is-an-at-the-money-option-5208335.

Probasco, J. (2021, February 10). Long Call Options Vs. Long Put Options - What 'Going Long' In Options Trading Means. Business Insider. https://businessinsider.com/markets/long-call-options-vs-long-put-options-what-going-long-in-options-trading-means/tsb1sz3.

Reuters. (2021, August 6). Japan Ends 300 Years Of Trading Rice Futures. Reuters. https://www.reuters.com/article/japan-rice-futures-idUSL4N2PD1Q2.

Segal, T. (2020, December 26). Intraday. Investopedia. https://www.investopedia.com/terms/i/intraday.asp.

Tastytrade. (2022). Glossary. Tastytrade. https://www.tastytrade.com/glossary.

Tastytrade. (2022). Implied Volatility In Options Trading: All You Need to Know. Tastytrade. https://www.tastytrade.com/concepts-strategies/implied-volatility.

Thakur, M. (2022). Difference Between Stock And Option. Wall Street Mojo. https://www.wallstreetmojo.com/stock-vs-option/.

www.ingramcontent.com/pod-product-compliance
Lightning Source LLC
Chambersburg PA
CBHW071433210326
41597CB00020B/3768